Poustinia

Christian Spirituality of the East
for Western Man

Catherine de Hueck Doherty

Collins
FOUNTAIN BOOKS

First published in 1975 by Ave Maria Press, USA
First issued in Fountain Books 1977
Second Impression June 1978

© 1975 Ave Maria Press, USA

Made and printed in Great Britain
by William Collins Sons & Co. Ltd Glasgow

Poustinia

Catherine de Hueck Doherty was born into a wealthy Russian family in 1900 and although brought up a Catholic was strongly influenced by the life of the Russian Orthodox Church. After the October Revolution of 1917 she and her ailing husband arrived penniless in Canada in 1920, and there Catherine had to work, gaining a first-hand knowledge of the life of the poor in North America.

Gradually her wealth grew once more, but with it her sense of vocation grew too, and finally she gave up her hard-won riches and returned to live amongst, and serve, the poor of Toronto. So was founded the first Friendship House. Others followed in the United States – in Harlem, Chicago, Washington and Portland. Then in 1947, back in Canada, Catherine and her second husband founded Madonna House, as a place of friendship, prayer and simple love. Now, 20 years later, she is still there and has made in it her own *poustinia*.

Contents

Introduction

There is no need to explain this book. It is written in simple words by a woman who has been speaking and writing about God for over 40 years. The power of her mind and her imagination, purified by faith and suffering and love, gives her words a clarity that ordinary people who are hungry for God understand at once. Yet there is a depth in the simple words of this book that the Lord himself has put there. He has shaped the words of Catherine de Hueck Doherty by shaping her life. Therefore we who belong to the community of Madonna House, which his Spirit has also shaped through her, thought it might be wise to say just a little about the context of her words—this life through which the Spirit has drawn our own lives so deeply into the love of Christ.

Catherine Kolyschkine was born into a wealthy family in Russia on the Feast of the Assumption, 1900. Her father was half Polish, and a Catholic, and thus she was reared as a Catholic. Yet it was the distinctively Russian incarnation of the gospel that she experienced in her childhood. Through the liturgy of the Russian Orthodox Church, the practices of living faith with which her parents filled their home, and the earthy piety of the Russian people themselves, sinners and skeptics as well as saints, Catherine received the great spiritual traditions and symbols of the Christian East. The sense of the world as the transfigured image of God; the awareness of the risen Christ, glorious and beautiful, yet humiliated still in the sufferings of the poor; the vision of the Church as immersed in and shining with the oneness of the Holy Trinity; and above all the passionate knowledge of the immense tenderness and mercy of God as the truth beyond every other truth—these formed Catherine, and they form every sentence of her book. Of course, all these traditions are also the heritage of the Catholic West, but in recent centuries the weeds of sectarian warfare and legalism, of Jansenism and secularism have often choked its growth. In Catherine's heart that good seed has grown essentially unhampered, as living and active in her as the love of her parents and the beauty of her native earth.

At 15 she was married to the Baron Boris de Hueck. After the October revolution of 1917, they lived through the terrors of Communist persecution and shared with all Russians the agonies of starvation and civil war. Finally they escaped with only the clothes on their backs and made their way to England. In 1920 they arrived in Canada, penniless and with a baby son to care for. The Baron's health had been shattered by the war, and Catherine, though not well herself, found what work she could to support the family. She was a maid, a laundress, a waitress, a salesclerk, and thus first came to know the people of North America by her friendships with the working poor of Toronto, Montreal, and New York.

Soon Catherine's energy and her gift for public speaking enabled her to find work with a lecture bureau. Within a few years she was one of its executives. Suddenly she was wealthy again. She had a large apartment, many books, a nurse for her son, a big car, important friends. Then in the midst of this new affluence she began to wonder if God had saved her from death in Russia only to make her a comfortable bourgeoise in North America. The words of Christ haunted her: "Sell all you possess, and give it to the poor, and come, follow me." It seemed madness, and she tried to close her soul to these words which she has described as sounding within her like the faint, disjointed stammerings of a dying man. She could not escape them, but when she went to priests for advice, they always told her that she was deluded, that her son was God's will for her.

In 1930, after several years of anguish, she went to the Archbishop of Toronto, Neil McNeil. He listened to her, then told her that she did indeed have a vocation from God. He asked her to pray for another year, after which he would give her his blessing and his support. A year later she sold everything she had, after providing for her son's education, and the young mother and her son went to live in the slums of a Toronto crippled by the Depression.

Catherine went simply to be with the poor, to love them and serve them very quietly, to become their friend, to pray with them and for them hidden in their midst. But when others saw her, they wanted to join her. Men and women flocked to her, in smaller numbers, but in the same way that people flock now to Mother Teresa in Calcutta. There was an intensity to her faith and to her love for the poor that lit a flame in the hearts of many. Her boldness and her strangeness, however, also scandalized others, and, after a few years, misunderstanding and calumny drove her out of Toronto. The first Friendship House was dead.

Soon, though, Father John LaFarge, S.J., arranged to have Catherine invited to New York to work in Harlem. She started Friendship House again, again alone in absolute poverty. Once again people came to share her life. The interracial apostolate grew in New York and expanded to other cities in the United States, to Chicago, Washington and Portland. Friendship House became well known, if not necessarily well thought of, in the American Church. She shared with her friend, Dorothy Day, the harsh struggle to move the social teachings of the Church out of books into people's hearts. Even if a few, such as the young Thomas Merton, recognized in her the power of the Holy Spirit and an unwavering fidelity to Christ's Church, many others were frightened by her Russianness or her bluntness. Others simply could not grasp the largeness of her vision, especially since her faith-experience differed so vastly from theirs. Because of a difference of opinion over the nature of the Friendship House Apostolate, Catherine found herself called to move again into the unchartered waters of the Lord.

This time, however, Catherine did not have to start over alone. Her first husband had long since died, and in 1943 she had married Eddie Doherty, the famous newspaperman. In 1947, then, she went with him and one of the Friendship House staff to Combermere, a little village 180 miles northeast of Toronto, where the Bishop of Pembroke had invited her to continue, somehow, her work. In bewilderment they came here, sure of nothing, yet on the day of their arrival they planted a small apple orchard. Somehow they knew that they had come home, and that the strange, dark vision of prayer, love, and simple service of the poor which the Lord had given Catherine would not be lost. They seemed to lack all human means to foster that vision, and often that first year they were tempted to leave. Still, they had planted those trees, and if they had come to what seemed to them a wilderness, they knew that it was the Lord's, and that he could make it bloom.

He did. Once again men and women came, and stayed, and this time priests came, and a few of them stayed too. The apostolate, now called Madonna House, grew slowly, and now, 27 years later, has 125 full-time members, including 14 priests. Madonna House has 12 missions, each of which in widely varied ways is a house of friendship, a place of prayer and simple love. Catherine and Eddie took a vow of celibacy in 1955, at the time when the community decided to establish itself more formally in the Church, though still keeping its lay character. Eddie was ordained a priest in the Melkite Rite in 1969, and, as this book shows, Catherine continues to speak and write to inspire not only the members of our own community, but thousands of others.

With the change of atmosphere brought by the Council and the resulting search for new forms of community and prayer, Catherine is respected now as a pioneer and spoken of with a kind of approval never given her since the beginning of her work. Madonna House might still look rather unusual to many, and Catherine more immutably Russian than ever, but I suspect that, horrified or intrigued by revolutions elsewhere within the Catholic Church, many people have decided that Catherine Doherty is far less radical than they once thought. Some may think that she can be indulged with respect now because in her old age she has become, at last, safe.

This book will show how false that belief is. It is true that she recognizes that many of her earlier battles have been won, or that others are carrying on her old struggles. It is true that she is not very interested in the kinds of reforms that preoccupy so many intelligent Catholics, but safe she is not. Comfortable she will never be. This book reveals the real scope of the vision that created the old Friendship House and the real source of that passionate zeal, that incredible energy of faith which has been the delight or the despair of all who have ever seen Catherine in action or heard her speak. In this book the radical wholeness of her life stands forth for all to see. If her life has shaped her words, her words now reveal her life. Her journey outward has always been also a journey inward, toward the fire of the living God burning in her heart. As she has moved, the Spirit has cast that fire about her on every side. Her pilgrimage has always been also a standing still in the center of her own heart, "where," she says, "all in me is silent and where I am immersed in the silence of God."

Catherine has heard that silence, and it has made her a free woman. She is still imperfect and sinful, but her freedom is the freedom won by the only true revolution the world has ever seen—the revolution of the gospel of the Son of God, who died and rose out of love for us to bring us out of the bondage of our isolation into communion as the children of his Father. The Lord Jesus led Catherine out of the peace of her childhood, through a terrible persecution, to a strange land and a strange calling, and he brought her to the *poustinia* of her own heart. There he has shared with her his own eternal childhood, and has filled her solitude with the men and women of the whole earth. In the silence of the Father he has given her his own words of life to speak.

These are the words Catherine speaks here. In writing about the poustinia, she is not writing so much about a technique of prayer as of a journey into God, her own and, if we want, ours. It is a journey filled with marvels and even terrors to be sure, but a journey open to all who want to take it. "Poustinia" sounds exotic, remote, yet Catherine shows that it is simply that secret room the Lord has told us of, where the Father will reward us with himself, in secret, if we only go there in faith. She tells us something of the treasures we will find there in God's Word—defenselessness, poverty, liberation. She shares with us her own knowledge of what it means to fight for the world at the center of that darkness that threatens to overwhelm the earth. She teaches us about beautiful gifts —tears, tongues of love, and especially the Jesus Prayer— that God will give us to heal the world's sickness. She reminds us of the hardest saying of all, that to live with Christ in his kingdom we must become as poor as he is. She reminds us too that his Mother stands with us in this place of poverty and weakness, to console us and to strengthen us with her "yes."

But most of all Catherine holds up to us a vision of "cosmic tenderness." In the desert God makes our hearts like the heart of his Son, gentle, lowly, compassionate. There we learn tenderness to all his creatures, to all our sisters and brothers, and, most important of all, to ourselves. It is when we know ourselves as the joy of God, images of the Lord Jesus, that our brothers and sisters become our joy. To my mind, this is the very core of Catherine's word to us. Mercy is the poustinik's, the Christian's, true availability to God and the children of God. Mercy is his fast, his work, his solitude, and his prayer, for love is the sacrifice God's Son offers for us. Thus when Catherine speaks of the Russian hope that at the end of time even the devil will be forgiven, she is not speculating on the nature of an angelic intellect, but affirming that the one omnipotent reality is the merciful love of God.

One of the most powerful of the stories about the fathers of the desert, those geniuses of the gospel life, tells of a meeting between Father Lot and Father Joseph. Father Lot asked what else he must do to be perfect. He said that he ate little, slept little, prayed without ceasing, worked always with his hands, and shared whatever he had with the poor. What, he wondered, did he lack? Then Father Joseph rose and stretched out his arms, and tongues of fire flashed from his fingers. "If you want," he said, "you can become a living flame." The fire of God, and whoever has faith to live only by his mercy will become a tongue of that fire.

Catherine Doherty has never wanted anything else and has never settled for anything less. She is, in all her human weakness, a living flame. Those of us who have been touched by the fire of God within her, enlightened by it and transformed by it, pray that each person who reads this book will touch that same fire. May the risen Lord lead each of you into the desert of your heart, and speak to you there in his Spirit, and show you there the radiant mercy of his Father's face. Then, may he lead you to his brothers and sisters who are everywhere awaiting your love.

Rev. Robert D. Pelton
Madonna House
Combermere, Ontario
June 11, 1974

A Word from the Author

Besides the fact that I have chosen a strange foreign word for the title of my book, I must also inform the readers that the first seven chapters were written in the early 60's.

Part II, written in 1973, was directed entirely to the dwellers in our poustinias who made this a life vocation.

Parts III and IV, written in the 70's, were factually addressed to the staff of Madonna House and are composed of my spiritual experiences in my own poustinia into which I go usually every Friday.

I felt that it was important for the reader to understand the sequence of the book.

In closing I want to tell you that all who read this book will be remembered in my humble prayers.

Catherine de Hueck Doherty

Part I

Poustinia

1

Silence . . . Desert . . . Prayer

Dan Herr, publisher of the *Critic*, once said, "Retreats are out . . . deserts are in!" Perhaps I am being presumptuous in thinking that his gentle little arrow was partially directed at me. For I haven't noticed too many other people on the North American continent writing about deserts or going to them.

For the last few years I have been talking and writing a great deal about silence, solitude, and deserts, and I will continue to write about them because I think they are vitally important to our growing, changing, technological, urban civilization. It is obvious that humanity is facing many problems, will have to face many more, and that these problems are deeply disturbing the souls of all men. It is just as certain that we cannot, must not, reject the new, strange, adventuresome, frightening world that is opening before us . . . that is already with us. Especially we Christians cannot do this because Christ has inserted himself into this world and we are his people, his body, and so we belong as he does to this world of IBM machines, to this world of cybernetics, that daily bring vaster problems before our minds, hearts and souls. For science moves faster and faster, so much faster than the men of today—or even the men of tomorrow—are able to apprehend, comprehend or assimilate.

Science continues to destroy, in its own relentless fashion, what might be called false myths, superstitions, and accretions that surround not only the Christian religion but even God himself, accretions which cling to the Church's robes. In one sense, science is doing a good job, and we should welcome its findings, always, however, appraising such findings in the light of the true revelation of the risen Christ.

This appraisal is so necessary especially in the age in which we live. So many people are going to seek Christ in so many places. He predicted as much: "Or, if people should tell you, 'Look, he's out in the desert!'—don't go there; or if they say, 'Look, he is hiding here!'—don't believe it" (Matt 24:26). The Fathers of the Church, the bishops, have been given graces by the Holy Spirit to make true appraisals. We must be watchful here.

Many "top secret" and as yet unpublicized findings of science have the power of making a robot out of man. It can, we are told, even change man himself genetically, or brainwash him into submission. At the same time, the world of science, together with the spiritual renewal, invite man (the center of creation) to an *experience* of a "liberty of the children of God" seldom known before.

Now, man can truly have an encounter with reality and rise to the very source—to the Origin that has no origin. For the mystery of men in the midst of the world, nature, technology, and urbanization is intrinsically a *Divine Mystery*. But it is still on the *cross* that God reveals himself to this scientific, technological civilization of ours. As usual, he is close and distant. As usual, he reveals himself through what is not himself, so that even modern man can recognize the fullness of truth—the image of God manifested in the world and its temporality.

But it is to be understood that this Mystery, first of all, is not found in the world as such. It is found and seized upon in the hearts of the men who seek him, without denying his existence. It is because man is fundamentally spirit—open to the absolute of the Divine—that he is always dissatisfied, in one manner or another, with all created reality. Nature is not divine. It is only a sign of God, a cry toward God.

It seems strange to say, but what can help modern man find the answers to his own mystery and the mystery of him in whose image he is created, is *silence, solitude— in a word, the desert.* Modern man needs these things more than the hermits of old.

If we are to witness to Christ in today's marketplaces, where there are constant demands on our whole person, we need silence. If we are to be always available, not only physically, but by empathy, sympathy, friendship, understanding and boundless *caritas*, we need silence. To be able to give joyous, unflagging hospitality, not only of house and food, but of mind, heart, body and soul, we need silence.

True silence is the search of man for God.

True silence is a suspension bridge that a soul in love with God builds to cross the dark, frightening gullies of its own mind, the strange chasms of temptation, the depthless precipices of its own fears that impede its way to God.

True silence is the speech of lovers. For only love knows its beauty, completeness, and utter joy. True silence is a garden enclosed, where alone the soul can meet its God. It is a sealed fountain that he alone can unseal to slacken the soul's infinite thirst for him.

True silence is a key to the immense and flaming heart of God. It is the beginning of a divine courtship that will end only in the immense, creative, fruitful, loving silence of final union with the Beloved.

Yes, such silence is holy, a prayer beyond all prayers, leading to the final prayer of constant presence of God, to the heights of contemplation, when the soul, finally at peace, lives by the will of him whom she loves totally, utterly, and completely.

This silence, then, will break forth in a charity that overflows in the service of the neighbor without counting the cost. It will witness to Christ anywhere, always. Availability will become delightsome and easy, for in each person the soul will see the face of her Love. Hospitality will be deep and real, for a silent heart is a loving heart, and a loving heart is a hospice to the world.

This silence is not the exclusive prerogative of monasteries or convents. This simple, prayerful silence is everybody's silence—or if it isn't, it should be. It belongs to every Christian who loves God, to every Jew who has heard in his heart the echoes of God's voice in his prophets, to everyone whose soul has risen in search of truth, in search of God. For where noise is—inward noise and confusion—there God is not!

Deserts, silence, solitudes are *not necessarily places but states of mind and heart*. These deserts can be found in the midst of the city, and in the every day of our lives. We need only to look for them and realize our tremendous need for them. They will be small solitudes, little deserts, tiny pools of silence, but the experience they will bring, if we are disposed to enter them, may be as exultant and as holy as all the deserts of the world, even the one God himself entered. For it is God who makes solitude, deserts, and silences holy.

Consider the solitude of walking from the subway train or bus to your home in the evening, when the streets are quieter and there are few passersby. Consider the solitude that greets you when you enter your room to change your office or working clothes to more comfortable, homey ones. Consider the solitude of a housewife, alone in her kitchen, sitting down for a cup of coffee before beginning the work of the day. Think of the solitudes afforded by such humble tasks as housecleaning, ironing, sewing.

One of the first steps toward solitude is a departure. Were you to depart to a real desert, you might take a plane, train or car to get there. But we're blind to the "little departures" that fill our days. These "little solitudes" are often right behind a door which we can open, or in a little corner where we can stop to look at a tree that somehow survived the snow and dust of a city street. There is the solitude of a car in which we return from work, riding bumper to bumper on a crowded highway. This too can be a "point of departure" to a desert, silence, solitude.

But our hearts, minds, and souls must be attuned, desirous, aware of these moments of solitude that God gives us. To be so attuned we must lose our superstition of time. God laughs at time, for if our souls are open to him, available to him, he can invite them, change them, lift them, transform them in *one instant!* He can say to someone driving that car bumper to bumper, "I will lead you into solitude and there I shall speak to your heart" (Hos 2:14).

There is no solitude without silence. True, silence is sometimes the absence of speech—but it is always the act of listening. The mere absence of noise (which is empty of our listening to the voice of God) is not silence. A day filled with noise and voices can be a day of silence, if the noises become for us the echo of the presence of God, if the voices are, for us, messages and solicitations of God. When we speak of ourselves and are filled with ourselves, we leave silence behind. When we repeat the intimate words of God that he has left within us, our silence remains intact.

Silence is truth in charity. It answers him who asks. But it must give only words filled with light. Silence, like everything else, either makes us give ourselves, or it becomes miserliness and avarice, in which we keep ourselves to ourselves. The scripture says that we will have to give an account for every word. Perhaps we may also have to render an account for the words that we have not spoken and should have!

Deserts, silence, solitude. For a soul that realizes the tremendous need of all three, opportunities present themselves in the midst of the congested trappings of all the world's immense cities.

But how, really, can one achieve such solitude? *By standing still!* Stand still, and allow the strange, deadly restlessness of our tragic age to fall away like the worn-out, dusty cloak that it is—a cloak that was once considered beautiful. The restlessness was considered the magic carpet to tomorrow, but now in reality we see it for what it is: a running away from oneself, a turning from that journey inward that all men must undertake to meet God dwelling within the depths of their souls.

Stand still, and look deep into the motivations of life. Are they such that true foundations of sanctity can be built on them? For truly man has been born to be a saint —a lover of Love who died for us! There is but one tragedy: not to be a saint. If these motivations of life are not such that they can be true foundations for sanctity, then the soul must start all over again and find other motivations. It can be done. It must be done. It is never too late to begin again.

Stand still, and lifting your hearts and hands to God, pray that the mighty wind of his Holy Spirit may clear all the cobwebs of fears, selfishness, greed, narrow-heartedness away from the soul: that his tongues of flame may descend to give courage to begin again.

All this standing still can be done in the midst of the outward noise of daily living and the duties of state in life. For it will bring order into the soul, God's order, and God's order will bring tranquillity, his own tranquillity. And it will bring silence.

It will bring the silence of a lover listening with all his being to the heartbeats of his beloved. The silence of a bride, who in her utter joy listens to her heart reechoing every word of the beloved. The silence of a mother, so deep, so inward, that in it she listens with her whole being to the voice of her children playing in a nearby yard, cognizant without effort, of the slightest change in each voice. Hers is a listening silence which takes place while she competently, efficiently and lovingly attends to her daily duties.

This silence will come and take possession also of lover, bride, mother, worker, nurse, apostle, priest, nun—if only the face of their soul, in the midst of their daily occupations, is turned to God.

At first such silences will be few and far between. But if nourished with a life of liturgical prayer, mental prayer, with the sacramental life of the Church, slowly, slowly, like the seedling of a mighty tree, silence will grow and come to dwell in a soul more and more often. Then suddenly, it will come to stay one day.

Then the soul will turn itself to its Beloved. Walking softly on this incandescent path of silence, he will come. His coming—once experienced—will make silence, henceforth, a precious thing. Now it will deepen, and, encompassing the whole man, will make man its own.

Yet, strangely enough, with silence dwelling constantly in the soul—a Mary of Magdala at the feet of Christ—speech will come more easily to people whose souls are completely recollected — in that silence — in the Lord. Speech and works too. They will move among men gently, softly, kindly. Love will shine in their every gesture, in their every word. There will always be time to do something more for someone, somewhere.

Nourished by the waters of silence, *caritas* will begin to sing its song of love, making all men and women literally spend themselves for others—at home, abroad, in any and every state of life, on all streets and marketplaces of the world. And lo! Behold. Their strength—even as their youth—will be renewed as an eagle's!

Slowly, imperceptibly, the world roundabout them will change. For the silence within them will become part of God's loving, mighty, creative, fruitful silence. His voice will be heard through them. His face will be seen in theirs! And the light of it will become a light to their neighbor's feet.

Thus silence will bring peace to all. The prayer of silence will be heard in our land far and wide. And the Beloved will once more come to dwell among men, for his vineyard—the world—will be restored to him. Yes, "Be still, and know that I am God" (Ps 46:10).

By the infinite grace of God, men and women of the

70's, having left behind them the "death of God," the
question of their "relevance or irrelevance," have now
turned their faces to prayer. Perhaps not only their faces,
but their minds and hearts and souls as well. The hungry
heart of man could not stand the terrible desert that surrounded it. It had to renew its contact with God—it had
to begin to pray again.

So, prayer is "in." Families talk about it. Young people
discuss it. Contemplative religious argue about it. All
religious orders are trying to understand it. Books that
teach about prayer in a variety of forms are best-sellers.
People pilgrim to find someone who can teach them how
to pray. People search for prayer houses, solitude, alone-
ness where they feel they can really pray. Yes, God's goodness once again reveals itself in this hunger for prayer and
in this hunger for communication with him. Once again
we realize that "without him we can do nothing."

But there is a danger here similar to the one discussed
above. Just as people fail to distinguish between silence
and physical solitude, so there is a danger not to distinguish
between prayer and solitude. These are two different aspects of the spiritual life. Prayer, of course, is the life of
every Christian. Without prayer, without contact with God,
this life dies. Solitude, on the other hand, is a special vocation; it is for the few, not the many. Yet, today, so
many are thinking of prayer houses and little places of
physical solitude. So many priests, sisters, brothers, whose
vocation is really an active one, suddenly have decided
that they can enter the solitude of a Carthusian monk. In
the majority of cases, this is just a daydream, a romantic
temptation of the spiritual life. Frankly, it is an escape
from the tensions that are holding priests, nuns, families,
and youth in a sort of unrelenting grasp these days. *Accept*,

first, the solitude of your own heart. Prayer, like silence, is a matter of a journey inward, as are all pilgrimages of the Spirit. I must journey inward to meet the Triune God that dwells within me.

To say all this may seem strange in the first chapter of a book which concerns, as you will soon see, a desert experience. But it is vitally important at the outset to emphasize that there is no need for a log cabin, cottages, huts, in order to lead a life of prayer. Prayer is interior. The hut, the log cabin, the chapel, is the human heart in which we must learn how to pray. Solitude sometimes helps prayer, and for special vocations is the cradle of prayer, and powerful prayer at that. But for the average Christian, prayer doesn't need a geographic spot. Prayer is a contact of love between God and man.

Married people don't need a bedroom to make love. One can make love anyplace, and "making love" does not necessarily mean immediately what people think it means! Making love can mean looking into each other's eyes. It can mean holding hands tightly. It means being aware of each other in the midst of a crowd. So it is with prayer. In the intense stillness of a loving heart all of a person strains toward the beloved, and words—simple, gentle, tender— come forth, audible or inaudible as the case may be.

To confuse prayer with solitude, to say that I must have solitude in which to pray, is a fallacy. It is good to have periodic solitude. Such is the plea of the present book. It is good to gather oneself up, to be awake with the Lord in Gethsemane, to watch not only one hour with him but perhaps more, all along the way of his Incarnation and on to Golgotha, on to the Resurrection, on to the bosom of the Father and the Spirit.

But this "solitude" requires only a small place. It can

be a room in a large convent or monastery. It can be a place in the attic or the basement of a family home. It may be a part of a room, separated by curtains. That would be a sufficient temporary solitude for simple recollection and greater peace. The daily noises of the street, of the family, of the staff of convents and monasteries would form a gentle reminder that we never pray alone, and never for ourselves alone.

Prayer is a full-time affair; solitude, unless called to a lifetime of it by God, must always be a temporary thing, lest it ceases to be solitude and becomes an escape. Unfortunately, the two are often mentioned in the same breath, whereas their roles in our lives with the Lord are different. Thanks be to God for the renewed desire to pray! But let us walk softly, and consult wise men, about our desire for solitude. It may be a grave temptation.

2

Poustinia and Poustinik

While firmly believing that silence and solitude are above all else attitudes of the mind and heart, I have for a long time now felt that we should be doing something more. Ours is a tragic century when men are faced with tremendous decisions that shake the souls of the strongest. This is also the age of neuroses, of anxiety, of fears, of psychotherapy, tranquilizers, euphoriants—all symbols of man's desire to escape from reality, responsibility and decision-making.

This is the age of idol-worship—status, wealth and power. The idols dominate the landscape like idols of old: they are squatty and fat. The First Commandment once again lies broken in the dust. The clouds of war, dark and foreboding—an incredible war of annihilation and utter destruction—come nearer. Dirge-like symphonies surround us and will not let us be.

What is the answer to all these darknesses that press so heavily on us? What are the answers to all these fears that make darkness at noon? What is the answer to the loneliness of men without God? What is the answer to the hatred of man toward God?

I think I have one answer—*the poustinia* (pronounced

"pou" as in "you"). Poustinia stands for prayer, penance, mortification, solitude, silence, offered in the spirit of love, atonement, and reparation to God! The spirit of the prophets of old! Intercession before God for my fellow-men, my brothers in Christ, whom I love so passionately in him and for him. It is not enough to lead a life of dedication and surrender as so many of the religious orders do. Every Christian must do more—with vows or without vows —wherever they are, whoever they may be!

That "more" can be a poustinia, an entry into the desert, a lonely place, a silent place, where one can lift the two arms of prayer and penance to God in atonement, intercession, reparation for one's sins and those of one's brothers. Poustinia is the place where we can go in order to gather courage to speak the words of truth, remembering that truth is God, and that we proclaim the word of God. The poustinia will cleanse us and prepare us to do so, like the burning coal the angel placed on the lips of the prophet.

The word "poustinia" is Russian meaning "desert." It is an ordinary word. If I were a little Russian girl, and a teacher during a geography lesson asked me to name a desert, I might say, "Saharskaya Poustinia"—the Sahara Desert. That's what it really means. It also has another connotation. as so many words have. It also means the desert of the Fathers of the Desert, who in ages past went away from everything and settled there. In the Western sense of the word, it would mean a place to which a hermit goes and, hence, it could be called a hermitage.

The word to the Russian means much more than a geographical place. It means a quiet, lonely place that people wish to enter, to find the God who dwells within them. It also means truly isolated, lonely places to which specially called people would go as hermits, and would seek God in solitude, silence and prayer for the rest of their lives!

However, a poustinia was not necessarily completely away from the haunts of men. Some people had reserved, in their homes, a small room to which they went to pray and meditate, which some might call a poustinia.

Generally speaking, however, a "poustinik" (a person dwelling in a poustinia) meant someone in a secluded spot. A poustinik could be anyone—a peasant, a duke, a member of the middle class, learned or unlearned, or anyone in between. It was considered a definite vocation, a call from God to go into the "desert" to pray to God for one's sins and the sins of the world. Also, to thank him for the joys and the gladness and all his gifts.

I got to be very familiar with one poustinik to whom my mother went for advice. I never knew who he was. We used to go there on foot and return on foot. When we arrived my mother knocked on the door and opened it. There was no latch on the door. The poustinik was always there to welcome anyone who came. Mother bowed to the cross that was prominent against the log wall, and to the icon of Our Lady. Then she would bow to the poustinik and say, "Peace be to this house," and he would say, "May the peace of the Lord be with you." I did the same. Then he would offer us some tea and some bread, whatever he had, and say, "Come and partake of what God in his mercy has sent me." Upon doing so, I went to play outside, and my mother talked to him. Then we went back home.

It is difficult to simply relate this man, and other poustiniks that I came to know through my lifetime, with what is called a "hermit." There was some kind of difference. The poustinik seemed to be more available. There was a gracious hospitality about him, as if he were never disturbed by anyone who came to visit him. On the contrary, his was a "welcome" face. His eyes seemed to sparkle with the joy of receiving a guest. He seemed to be a listening person. A person of few words, but his listening was deep, and there was a feeling that he understood. In him St. Francis' prayer seemed to become incarnate: he consoled, he understood, and he loved—and he didn't demand anything from anyone for himself.

He was available in other ways. If someone from the village was in need (for instance, if a farmer needed his hay in before the rain), he rushed over to the poustinik and asked his help. The poustinik immediately dropped everything and went with the farmer. He was always available.

Usually the poustinik was a man, though there were women poustinikki also. Sometimes they were single people, sometimes they were widows and widowers. Not all of them were educated in the academic sense of the word. Quite often they were just ordinary peasants, but usually they had what we call "letters," that is to say, they could read and write. Amongst the "staretzi"—the old and wise ones —could even be found the nobility. It is said that one of the czars, Alexander I, went into a poustinia. There is a mystery about the many years of his absence, so they say.

Whoever these people were, they were not necessarily old in age. In Russia, the "old one," *staretz* (or *staritza* for a woman) means "wise one." Usually they were people who went into the poustinia around the age of 30 or 35. Others may have been older, in their late 50's or early 60's, who had been married, reared their children, and then felt the attraction of the desert. But the majority of the lay people were around 30 to 40 years old.

There was no big fuss about going into a poustinia. From some village, from some nobleman's house, from some merchant's house—from any part of our society in Russia—a man would arise. (Of course, only God knows *why* he did arise.) He would arise and go into the place (as the Russians say) "where heaven meets earth," departing without any earthly goods, usually dressed in the normal dress of a pilgrim. In summertime, this garb was a simple handwoven shift of linen of the kind that ladies wear these days, only it came down to his or her ankles. It was tied in the middle with an ordinary cord. He took along a linen bag, a loaf of bread, some salt, a gourd of water. Thus he or she departed, after, of course, taking leave of everyone in the household or in the village. Some didn't even do this. They just stole away at dawn or in the dark of the night, leaving a message that they had gone on a pilgrimage and maybe would find a poustinia to pray to God for their sins and the sins of the world, to atone, to fast, to live in poverty, and to enter the great silence of God.

There were other poustinikki, both men and women, who had been monks and nuns of an order. Since Russian orders are contemplative in the Western sense, these people would get permission from their abbots or abbesses to become poustinikki, dwellers of the poustinia and the desert. Since some of the real estate holdings of the monasteries were large, which often included much wild and uncultivated land, it would not be difficult to find a place where they could build themselves a poustinia, or have one built for them if they were women. Also, they might simply be given permission to go and find their desert for themselves. In this case, they would go on a pilgrimage to a holy place, pray there, and get some inspiration as to where to go. Or, they might just simply walk around prayerfully until they found a place. Yet, there were a variety of poustinikki or dwellers of the desert—*startzi* or *stapooha* as we call them

P.

in Russia. Women were in the minority; usually they began to dwell in the poustinia in their old age.

My father had a friend, his name was Peter. He was well-born, of the nobility, the eldest son of an old Russian family. He was pretty close to what is called in America a millionaire. He had a lot of gold and silver in the bank, besides having real estate and so forth. One day he came to my father and said, "Theodore, I have been reading the gospels and I have decided, as so many before me, to accept them literally." My father listened. He continued: "I am going to gather my goods, especially my gold and silver. I am leaving my farms, my real estate to my family, but my money in the bank I am changing literally into silver and gold pieces." This he did, and my father accompanied him through the whole transaction.

In those days there were no trucks. There were what we called drays that carried what today trucks carry. They were pulled by two horses. My father said that it was a big dray, perhaps the equivalent of a one- or one-and-a-half-ton truck. It was filled with sacks, and the sacks contained gold and silver. Peter, with my father accompanying him, went to the poor section they call the slums now of Petrograd. There, family by family, house by house, Peter gave away his pieces of gold and silver. When the dray was empty Peter said: "Now, I have in some small measure ransomed the 30 pieces of silver for which God was sold. And now I must go."

So they returned to his house where, on his bed, there was laid out a linen tunic. He took a linen bag, a loaf of bread, and in another little linen bag he took some salt. He also had a gourd of water and a staff. On foot, my father walking with him, he went through the streets of Petrograd. My father accompanied him to the outskirts of the city and into the country roads. The last he saw of him was just a silhouette against the setting sun—a man in a long garment with a staff in his hand. He had no cash in his pockets (he had no pockets), nor in his bag. He had only some bread, water, salt, and a staff. Not even shoes. That was all.

Years later, my father chanced to be in Kiev, which was a large city in the south of Russia. He went to Mass and, as was the custom in those days, all the beggars assembled on the church steps before Mass to beg from the good people who went in. Amongst them was a man with a beard, matted and seemingly uncombed, long hair, and tattered garments. He looked like a fool, a retarded person. His eyes were vacant, no expression on his face, except the one usually associated with retarded people or idiots. But a ray of sun came out and fell on his face—and my father recognized his friend Peter! He called out his name and intelligence returned to that face. They embraced. They went to Mass together and then had breakfast. My father asked, "Why have you chosen this vocation of idiot or retarded person?" Peter answered, "I am atoning for the men who have called Christ a fool during his lifetime and during all the centuries thereafter." They kissed each other again, and Peter disappeared. My father never saw him again.

Peter had belonged to the *jurodivia*. These were a group of people who lived with the poor, totally poor themselves, begging their alms at church doors and street corners. They fasted. One might say that they stood side by side with the poustinikki, for these latter too, though living in abject poverty, lived alone, prayed, and listened. But their vocation and their goal was atoning for one thing and one thing only: for men once upon a time having called God a "fool."

Because men continue to call God a fool, the *jurodivia*

feel they have a continuous vocation of poverty, atonement and prayer—like the poustinik, yet different from him.

Then there were the pilgrims who constantly criss-crossed Russia carrying their poustinias in their hearts, sleeping under the trees, in haylofts, wherever they were allowed to. They were poor, alms-begging people, praying for the whole world constantly.

These spiritual traditions still go on. For when I was in Rome in 1967 for the International Lay Congress, I had occasion to translate for four Russian theologians. They spoke neither French nor English, so I had to translate back and forth for them.

We became very well acquainted. I asked them: "Are the Russians still pilgrimaging?" They just looked at me and said, "Do you think communism can stop pilgrimaging in Russia?" I felt like falling through the floor! Nevertheless, I asked another question along the same lines: "And what about the poustinikki?" They answered that the forests were still full of poustinias and poustinikki, and that even the communists were known to go into the forests to look for the poustinikki—and somehow or other remain there! But, they added, these were unconfirmed reports.

Perhaps we (Russians) as a nation have been chosen for this somewhat strange vocation—lest the world forget about the essence of our faith, which is above all to render glory to God. The essence of our faith is to eternally seek to know God better in order to glorify him more and to serve him better in men.

We Russians tend to identify ourselves especially with the poor, and so to be cold, to be homeless, to be pilgrims for those who have no holy restlessness and who don't want to arise and seek God. All this seems quite natural to us. So many of us feel that the rest of men are looking for him where he cannot be easily found—in the comfortable life which is in itself not sinful, but which can become a sort of asphyxiation and isolation from the rest of mankind. Comfort can become an idol too.

So these strange vocations are the vocations of my people and of many other peoples who follow the Eastern spirituality.

3

The Eastern Poustinik

Who were these men and women of Russia and why did they go into "the desert," into the poustinia? I have already explained, or tried to, *who* they were, meaning that they came from all strata of society—nobility, merchant, peasant, middle class. But what should interest us now is what they were like interiorly. Who were they spiritually?

They were people who craved in their hearts to be alone with God and his immense silence. Why did they crave that silence, that solitude? For themselves? No. A hermit of this type, according to the Eastern spirituality, went into the poustinia *for others*. He offered himself as a holocaust, a victim for others.

The mountain of God's silence—covered with the cloud of his mysterious presence—called these future poustinikki in that awesome yet loving way.

To go into the poustinia means to listen to God. It means entering into *kenosis*—the emptying of oneself. This emptying of oneself, even as Christ emptied himself for us, is really a climbing of this awesome mountain right to the very top where God abides in his warm silence.

It also means to know "how terrible it is to fall into the hands of the living God" . . . and yet how delightful, how joyful, and how attractive! So attractive, in fact, that the soul cannot resist. That is why the Russians say that he who is called to the poustinia must go there or die because God has called him to this mountain to speak to him in that awesome silence, in that gentle, loving silence!

For God has something to say to those whom he calls to the poustinia, and what God says to them the poustinikki must repeat as a prophet does.

Humanly and psychologically speaking he is reluctant to speak, as every prophet was reluctant; but to him too comes the angel with the coal of fire, that invisible angel that cleanses his mind, his mouth, and his lips (symbolically speaking) and watches the man or woman arise and start on this awesome pilgrimage.

The Russian pilgrims of old went with provisions for only one day, as Christ told his disciples to do. Thus the first step outside his house, wherever that house, apartment, village or cabin may be, was always a momentous step, for these people truly left all things, not only father and mother, brothers and sisters, and often even wives and children, but they also left the life of their community, of their family, of their village, and of all their social relationships.

They went forth alone . . . alone, into the unknown! Yes, the individual lay man or woman who was called to the poustinia went into it to be truly alone, alone physically with God. They emptied their minds and their souls of all their relationships because from now on they would be with all their loved ones in a new relationship, in a deeper dimension of love. For those who leave everything for God receive everything back from him, but in a different way.

They are the ones of whom it can be said that they have learned "how to care and not to care"! From now on the poustinikki would live with all those whom they had left behind in the great silence of God. They would be constantly lifted up to the face of God. Yes, they had to learn to care and not to care.

But what is the silence of God but the speech of the Lord? The Father speaks through the Son who is his Word, and the Holy Spirit echoes both Three in One and One in Three. It is to meet *them* that these men and women left everything and everyone.

From the moment their poustinia was built, from the moment of their closing its door upon themselves, not only they but the whole of humanity entered into that cabin with them.

It is for all this the poustinik was to pray, to weep, to endure all the temptations that come to him who lives in the desert. It was for *them* that he was to mortify his flesh, for *them* that he accepted the loneliness that transcends our understanding, and which at the same time, once accepted, is no real loneliness at all.

When he closed the door for the first time he entered the very essence of the novitiate of God's love, for in this wondrous, extraordinary, awesome, beautiful, tremulous silence of God he would learn to know who God is.

God would reveal himself to the poustinik in a fullness that he rarely communicates even to those who live in a religious community.

But, of course, who am I to judge to whom God reveals himself more or reveals himself less? It is a question we must leave for God to answer, but this is the belief of Eastern spirituality.

The more I try to explain the poustinia and the Russian idea of it, the more I find myself floundering. I find it an exceedingly difficult task because what I speak about is so very foreign to the Western mind of today, especially to those on the North American continent. Yet I know that the poustinia is at least one answer for this Western culture which depends so much on cerebration, intellectualism, and having a need to sift everything through the mind and examine everything with almost scientific precision.

So if there is anything that can help to rectify the defects of such a mentality it is precisely the poustinia experience of the Eastern spirituality. For it is neither Eastern nor Western but simply Christian. It is the eternal hunger of men for God whom they seek whether they know it or not as pilgrims of the Absolute.

Every man is a pilgrim on the road of life. Some—and there are more than we know of—are like the poustinikki, truly seeking the Absolute—God!

So I think the poustinia will begin slowly to attract many such people who will arise now here, now there, across the vast North American continent, and go seeking to find a place where they can enter into the silence of God and meet his Word—Christ—in that silence.

I hope that I have given you some idea of what a poustinia meant to some Russians and how it was open to everyone, learned or unlearned, male or female, though the inspiration to arise, seek it, and enter into it came from God.

Those who were called to this vocation (or perhaps were tormented by it before they understood it) had to be blessed by a priest of the Church. No Russian would go forth on his own without going to Mass, partaking of the bread and wine, and receiving the blessing of a priest.

It must be acknowledged that though both men and women arose, the majority of them were men who left all they had. Some had little and some had much, but that really doesn't matter. They left it to enter the poustinia as a lifetime vocation or at least one that was to last many years.

They entered it with empty hands. They sought the knowledge of God directly, not through book knowledge, for they didn't believe that God revealed himself through books.

The poustinik, the dweller in the poustinia, the *staretz*, the hermit—to call him by the many names that the Russians use—begins with the idea that there is only one book that can teach him God. He believes that the only way to know God is to go to him in humility, simplicity and poverty, entering his silence, and there in prayer and patience waiting until he reveals himself according to his own good timetable.

So into the poustinia the poustiniks brought one book only—the bible. They read it on their knees, impervious or even perhaps uninterested in any purely academic question. To them the bible was the incarnation of the Word and they felt a lifetime wasn't enough in which to read it. Every time they opened it they believed with a tremendously deep faith that they were face to face with the Word.

Yes, the poustinik reads the bible on his knees. He doesn't read with his head (conceptually, critically) except in the sense that the words pass through his intelligence, but the intelligence of the poustinik is in his heart. The words of the bible are like honey on his tongue. He reads them in deep faith. He doesn't analyze them. He reads them and allows them to stay in his heart. He may read only one or two sentences or maybe a single page in one day. The point is that he puts them all in his heart like Mary did. He lets them take root in his heart and waits for God to come and explain them which he inevitably will do when he finds such deep and complete faith.

When Mary was greeted by the angel she didn't totally understand what the greeting meant or what the result would be. She simply said *"Fiat,"* "Yes." Neither did she understand what Christ said to her in the temple after three days of looking for him. Yet, she "put all his words into her heart" and that is what a Russian poustinik will do too. He will put them there, keep silent, waiting for God to take those words out of his heart and reveal to him what those words mean.

Thus the hermit, the poustinik, learns to know God. Not learn *about* him, but learn *of God himself through God himself.*

For in the tremendous silence into which this poustinik entered, God reveals himself to those who wait for that revelation and who don't try to "tear at the hem of a mystery" forcing disclosure.

No, the poustinik lies prostrated, waiting for God to explain, as God did to the disciples of Emmaus, whatever God wants to explain to him. All he knows is that his heart too will burn within him as did that of those disciples.

The person who follows the call to the poustinia and who leaves everything behind relies on the help of his fellow-men. He becomes in reality a beggar. In Russia, when a village knew that a hermit was going to dwell in some abandoned hut or one that he would come to beg them help to build, they were glad. It meant that there was someone praying for them. So the poustinik usually selected a se-cluded spot in a clearing in the woods. The hermit really sought the hidden places of his world—mountains, forests, woods—places where he was really alone with God. Thus his human horizons were somewhat limited so that his spiritual horizons could grow without distraction.

His food supply was taken care of. He usually had a vegetable garden, fished in some stream or river, cut wood for his stove to keep himself warm in the winter, and tried to earn a living. He also occupied himself with some work, like weaving baskets which he didn't sell but gave away to people who needed them. People came to visit him, many did. For a Russian hermit has no lock or latch on his door except against the wind. Anyone at any time of day or night can knock at his door. Remember, he is in the poustinia not for himself but for others. He is a connecting bridge between men and God and God and men, and God speaks through him especially when people have need of the alms of God's word—the alms of God's mercy, tenderness, compassion, understanding, reassurance—who doesn't need these things almost all the time! The East believes that the poustinik is such a channel so they come to him and he must always be available.

He also must share the food with anyone that comes. They may refuse, but it must always be offered. He may just have a piece of bread, but he will break it in half or into as many parts as there are people. Thus the second aspect of this strange life is hospitality . . . the sharing of what he has . . . the offering of it at any given moment. Hospitality above all means that the poustinik is just passing on whatever God has put into his empty hands. He gives all that he has and is: words, work, himself, and his food.

What does it mean when we say he gives of his works? Let us say that he lives not far away from a village and there is a lot of hay to be brought in. The sky is dark and it looks as if a storm were moving in. Quickly someone is dispatched to the poustinik who tells him, "Brother, the villagers need you to cut the hay."

Immediately the poustinik drops everything or anything he might be doing—prayer, garden, reading, whatever it may be—and spends all his time on the hay.

For we believe in Russia that if I touch God I must touch man, for there is really no distinction. Christ incarnated himself and became man, so I must, like Christ himself, be a person of the towel and the water. That is to say, wash the feet of my fellowmen as Christ did, and washing the feet of my fellowmen means service.

I cannot pray if I don't serve my brother. I cannot pray to the God who incarnated himself when my brother is in need. It is an impossibility. It would be like the priest, the Levite, who passed the man beset by robbers, and that one cannot do.

So sometimes a poustinik might spend a month, six weeks, working for the various needs of the villagers and never think even for one minute about the fact that he is supposed to be in a poustinia, reading the bible, praying or what-have-you, because *he is in the poustinia of his heart always,* especially when serving his fellowmen.

Another aspect of the poustinik's life is mortification. The poustinik is a mortified person. The Russians believe that you must lift the two arms of prayer and penance to God. The prayer that the poustinik prays constantly is the Jesus Prayer.† Besides that he is, of course, free to pray any other prayer he wants to, like for instance the Akathist* of Our Lady, but the Jesus Prayer is the prayer of the poustinik. But besides praying he must also mortify his body, especially by fasting.

If you ever see a *sad* hermit or poustinik, then he is no hermit at all. The most joyful persons in Russia are the ones who have the eyes of a child at 70 and who are filled with the joy of the Lord: the poustinikki, for they who

---

† "Lord Jesus Christ, Son of the living God, have mercy on me, a sinner."

* An Eastern devotional service in honor of Our Lady. The word literally means "not sitting" as the congregation stands throughout.

have entered the silence of God are filled with God's joy.
So if you ever see a sad poustinik he is a hypocrite and a
liar. Yes, the life of a poustinik should be truly joyous with
the quiet joy of the Lord and this will be visible. He will
have the eyes of a child even if his face is that of an old
woman or man. You cannot fool people as to such things
as the presence of love and joy in a human being.

So the poustinik is a man of mortification and penance.
But there is also a belief in the Eastern spirituality that the
poustinik may be called out of the poustinia by God. He
will know that moment. How? The Russian doesn't analyze
it but accepts it on faith. Usually it is said that the poustinik
can leave the poustinia when he has ceased to know that
he is praying and then it is time to go like Christ the
preacher to prophesy; that is to say, to tell that which God
has imparted to him in his great silence.

Then the poustinik becomes a pilgrim again. He doesn't
return to his native place, to his people, though he might
pass among them. He becomes a pilgrim who tells what
he has heard to all those whom he meets, making sure that
all those he meets understand that these are not his words
but the words he has heard in the silence of God, in the
poustinia, and that God commissioned him to bring these
words to the world. In this way two strange Russian vocations blend. A pilgrim may become a poustinik; a poustinik may become a pilgrim. The pilgrim who becomes
a poustinik was a searcher, trying to find out a little more
deeply where God wanted him. The poustinik who leaves
the poustinia and becomes a pilgrim is a prophet and his
vocation is settled. He doesn't pilgrim now to find out what
his vocation may be. He comes now to speak the words
of God.

There are some who are pilgrims for life. There are

some poustinikki who die in their poustinia. In most cases, however, they have achieved a Christian maturity which was prepared for them by God and given to them by God through his silence in their solitude. Now they can go and proclaim what they have heard in their great silence.

Let us hope that sometime in our lives we might meet such people.

4

Beginnings at Madonna House

For years after I left Russia, I didn't think a poustinia (in the terms in which I just described it) could possibly be even attempted in the West, let alone lived out. As far as my personal life had been concerned, the desire for silence and solitude hadn't left me just because I had crossed an ocean. From the very beginning of my life in this new world I sought silence and solitude in my own fashion.

My seeking mostly took the shape of going to convents for private retreats. I would go to one, and after the usual amenities were over, I would immure myself in my room. I spent my time between the chapel and that room. It wasn't often that I could get away to do this for a weekend or a Sunday. I had my family and later the work of the Apostolate to take care of.

But even before this time, when the question of my own vocation had been insistently pressing itself upon me, I had begun to think about again, or shall I say "resurrect," this old idea of poustinia among my people. I wondered if it was possible to incarnate it in this Western, American, technological society.

I had recourse to the bible. Whenever I opened it I always found the words, "Arise — go! Sell all you possess

. . . give it directly, personally to the poor. . . ." Thus, at a certain point in my life I decided to sell what I possessed, give it to the poor, and according to the ways of my people, go "into the people" and become a poustinik, spending half a day in prayer and half a day in serving the Lord in my neighbor. I was able to achieve this style of life for a very short while in Toronto, Ontario, Canada.

I had a little room. I had solitude, and I had the poor, and all this was done with the blessing and approbation of Archbishop Neil McNeil of the diocese.

All went well for a very little while until three girls and two young men came and desired to join me! I hadn't planned to start any kind of community, group, organization, or what have you. But the Archbishop asked me to accept them. Slowly, we became a spiritual family which today is know as the Madonna House Apostolate. It was composed first of men and women, and later of men, women and priests.

Those early days were the days of the depression, followed almost immediately by World War II. The accent in Canada and America was on social action, labor problems, on the ghetto, on interracial justice. Such action was so obviously needed that no one could deny its need. So, our lay apostolic family (in those days called Friendship House) was engaged in all these activities, though prayer was always a part of our lives. As I said, we eventually called our apostolate Madonna House, and its headquarters was located in Combermere, Ontario, Canada. Then, in 1961, I started thinking again about poustinia.

Many thoughts about Russian spiritual traditions kept coming back to me. It was as if I had kept a lot of words in my heart that I had heard from my people. I had laid them carefully aside, evidently wrapped up in the linen of memories, and perhaps I was afraid to unwrap them. I was afraid because I was living in a culture, a land, a civilization that seemed to be too far removed from such spiritual traditions. However, sometimes God unwraps the linens that contain memories and brings them forth to look at, to meditate upon, and to pray about.

It is said that "God writes straight with crooked lines," and sometimes I believe it to be true. So far as I was concerned, the lines that he brought forth from my heart were straight, but their implementation appeared to me to be crooked, and, frankly, I really thought these traditions were inapplicable in the West.

But who was I to say that what God brought forth from my soul was inapplicable? So I kept praying about it. One day I was walking near one of our farms located on a hill, and I came upon a farmhouse. It was old, beautifully shingled, and in good condition. I looked around and really noticed how beautiful the scenery was, for the fields of that farm were surrounded by woods that slowly sloped down that hill into the distance.

I walked away from the house and looked at it again and suddenly I stood very still because I realized that God wasn't really writing straight with crooked lines for me. He was writing straight with straight lines, and the end of the straight line was that house I was looking at!

It could . . . it just possibly could be transformed into becoming the first poustinia of Madonna House!

Strange how the memory of yesterday became suddenly the reality of today at that moment. I walked up to the house, opened the door, and stepped inside. It was a simple farmhouse with one big room, evidently the family kitchen, and next to it another room. There was a little stairway going upward and leading into the second floor, and three small bedrooms.

Slowly I again descended the stairway and went out-side, but then I returned and sat on the little steps of the front door that I kept open, looking now inside the house, now outside.

I must have spent a long time there, for I really had to face what to me was a danger zone; not necessarily physical danger, but emotional danger; for what in heaven's name was I dreaming about when I wanted to change this farmhouse into a poustinia?

It was truly a spiritual matter that I was dealing with— deeply spiritual. I was about to bring the fruit of another country, another civilization, another background, into this new land! Who would understand it? How could I present it to them? I must have spent a long time there for I sud-denly realized that the sun was setting behind the hills and the woods. So I arose, closed the front door, and slowly wended my way down the overgrown path to the country road where I had parked my car and returned to Madonna House, full of wonderment, some fears, and a listening heart, for most assuredly this was a time to listen to God.

Days passed, weeks passed, and months passed, and I kept praying and listening, and then one day I felt I had to bring this matter up before our family because it became very clear to me that God wanted a poustinia on the North American continent. But I felt that this wasn't a decision that I could make alone or impose on the community.

So I began with the community of Madonna House. We went back to the farm and the shingled house again and again. I would bring a little group or a large group to look it over and began to explain slowly, perhaps a little haltingly, but nevertheless joyfully, the idea of a poustinia to all of them.

Later I began to write about it to those members of our family who were in the missions. Another thing that helped to clarify the matter was the fact that I was able to show the place and the house to all the local directors who came for their annual meeting in September, 1962.

The members of our spiritual family were interested, there is no denying that, but I realized that there was quite a bit of incomprehension as to what it was all about. I also realized that it would take time to really allow this to penetrate deeply into the minds, souls and hearts of everyone connected with Madonna House.

It was at this point I began to write letters on the poustinia, because I believed that many Christians in both Canada and America still did not know too much about this concept of poustinia that came from my land. I want to share with you the letters I wrote to the members of our family. They are part of the historical development of the poustinias in Madonna House but they are also part of God suddenly putting flesh on the memories that I had so carefully put away in my heart. Not only putting flesh on them but bringing them forth for all to see.

I wrote. "The poustinia must be almost stark in its simplicity and poverty. It must contain a table and a chair. On the table there must be a bible. There should also be a pencil and some paper. In one corner are a basin and pitcher for washing up. The bed, if bed there be, should be a cot with wooden slats instead of a mattress, a couple of blankets or quilts and a pillow if absolutely necessary. This is all that should be offered in the way of bedding. Drinking water, a loaf of bread, which will be divided into three parts, one for breakfast, one for lunch and one for dinner. For those who are not accustomed to eating their bread with water, there are the makings for tea and coffee.

"Prominent in the poustinia is a cross without a corpus, about six feet by three feet, which is nailed to the wall, and an icon of Our Lady in the eastern corner with a vigil light in front of it. The cross without a corpus is a symbol of one's own crucifixion on it, for those of us who love Christ passionately want to be crucified with him so as to know the joy of his resurrection.

"So much for the physical setup of the poustinia or desert.

"But of course there is so much more than the physical aspect of a place like that. The desert, of course, is the symbol of austerity, poverty, and utter simplicity. It is God who leads the soul to the desert and the soul cannot remain in the desert long unless it is nourished by God. Therefore, it is a place where we fast from bodily food and even spiritual food, such as reading all kinds of books, for we enter there to meet our God with the only book in which he is fully accessible: the bible.

"Now let us think over what I have said, first, about the physical setup of the poustinia and, secondly, about the spiritual approach to it. I would like to know your reactions to that letter.

"Probably you got quite curious and a little bit emotionally involved in it, or at least you were when we went up to that farm and that house to wash and paint it.

"I can understand that very well, for indeed it is such a new and exciting idea that it must involve people emotionally, intellectually, and spiritually—every which way, in fact. But let me warn you, for I have gone into the desert many, many times; like Christ you will find it also a fearsome place.

"Yet I don't mean a place to be afraid of, but a place where fear will come in occasionally and dwell with you—

the kind of fear every man experiences in the soul, for as far as the devil is concerned and my knowledge of him, if there is anything the devil detests it is the poustinia.

"However, at first, being in the poustinia will be exciting. As you repeat the experience, say one day a month, month after month, you will soon understand, and a great spiritual travail will take place in your soul. You will experience boredom, spiritual dryness. Time, at times, will seem very long. That, incidentally, is one of the reasons why you will not be allowed to go into it for more than 24 hours at first, and maybe with the permission of your spiritual director, for 36 or 48 hours.

"At all costs the desert must be a place of utter simplicity, as I have already explained. No books, no curtains, no pictures, except for an icon. And don't let us kid ourselves into thinking a poustinia must always be in the country, must always be a log house, or a shingled farmhouse as we happen to have in Madonna House. No, this would be a false idea of the poustinia—the desert—for the desert, the poustinia, can be located everywhere, for fundamentally it is interiorized. If you have a spare room in the house or a large closet, it will do.

"Truly the desert will strip you. The Lord of the Desert will do that too. Truly you will be tempted even as he had been tempted. You will suffer as he has suffered, but you will also be filled with tranquillity—the tranquillity of God's order.

"It is to be remembered that you are going to the desert for the following reasons:

To fast
To live in silence
To pray

So that you might die to yourself
quicker, so that Christ might grow in
you faster. So that you might give
him to the world faster too . . . this
world that is so hungry for him.
To atone for your sins and those of
others
To pray for mankind
To pray for peace
To pray for the missions and unity
among Christians in the Catholic Church
To become saints faster *i.e.*, lovers of
Christ in truth and in deed
To imitate Christ
To save your soul and that of others
To learn total surrender to God quicker
We have made Christ wait long enough.

"Consider these points, dearly beloved, consider why you go there, and prepare your soul for that going and that dying for Christ's sake so as to be resurrected for his sake too."

A second letter. "As I promised you in my last letter, I will continue to try to explain to you the spirit of the desert and the approach to it, for it is indeed a most important move that Madonna House has made in its history (this integration of the desert experience), though you might not realize it.

"The eternal paradox of Christ and his Church continues. On the one hand, Mother Church seems to relax everything with the relaxation of rules regarding fast and abstinence but, on the other hand, the Pope is calling with great urgency on the whole family of God who are of good will to engage themselves in every work of penance and good work possible before the Lord.

"A contradiction? Perhaps, yet when you think it over, it isn't, for Mother Church understands that in our frantic age of rat races, cold and hot wars, insecurity, fast transportation with its sudden change of climate, that all such things demand an abolition of the rigid fasting restrictions. For modern man isn't like his ancestors were, living mostly a rural, secure, well-rooted, peaceful existence.

"But on the other hand, this removal of official restrictions of food liberates the human person and opens wide the door of his love for Christ, the door to his understanding of the *kenosis* that he must undergo (the emptying of himself so as to be filled with Christ). It leaves the road clear for his dying to self through the use of his own free will, his love, his generosity, and his understanding of what is involved.

"Having thus liberated the faithful, the Pope now calls on their own love of God and the Church to do *more* than was asked before. It is no paradox, you see, once approached simply in the truth of the Holy Spirit.

"I was struck too that the idea of the poustinia for our Madonna House family came to me quite a while before the Pope wrote his encyclicals on penance. So you might say that at this moment Madonna House is completely in tune with the mind of God, his holy Church and bride, and his vicar on earth. A good place to be.

"Let us clarify a little further. I didn't expect everyone immediately to get their turn in the poustinia or to desire to get it. It will have to be a combination of your heart listening to God, finding out his will about it, and then checking with your spiritual director, for at all times before one goes to the poustinia one must check with one's spiritual director. Should he refuse, you must accept that refusal too with a great peace of mind. Eventually the time will come when his permission will be forthcoming. These are the dispositions needed for everyone who wishes to enter the desert of God. For if they enter of their own will exclusively they will not be qualified because God will disqualify them.

"Let your poustinia be a quiet, secret garden enclosed, for it is a hallowed place, a holy place where the soul enters to meet its God. It is not a showplace to be discussed or shown off."

Here is my next letter on the poustinia.

"You understand, I hope, why God brought forth those memories from my soul, clothed them with flesh, and made them a reality. When I contemplated for the first time that shingled house amidst the hills and forest, I was worried about you—all of you.

"So slowly, slowly, the idea of the poustinia 'took' in Madonna House, though not yet in our urban missions and the marketplace. It seemed as if the marketplace had come to Madonna House with the constantly growing influx of young people who kept passing through it in search of answers. All of us here opened our hearts and our house to them, for this is what we call true hospitality—the hospitality of the heart and of the house. But after the summer and the great holidays of the year, the entry into the great silence of God seemed to me to be a necessity.

"Our staff slowly got used to the idea and also began to see it as a necessity. The shingled house was used for the first year by the staff only. Slowly, very slowly, the idea began to spread to our missions. Some found corners or rooms that they could use in their houses. Others built little shacks; others used empty rooms in convents or retreat houses; and I hoped that someday each of our houses would have a real poustinia of its own. However, that lies in the future."

Meanwhile, a most strange phenomenon took place. As we began housing our poustinia in that farmhouse, our visitors became interested and our lonely poustinia became a very popular place. Everybody wanted to go there. The list of people wanting to enter the poustinia grew and grew until we realized we had to build more poustinias and this we did, even building a poustinia for me on my island. Notwithstanding the growth of our poustinias, there was always a long line of people wanting to get into them, and this continued all during the year. Because so many priests and nuns wanted to avail themselves of these poustinias, we built another poustinia by the priests' house.

To be absolutely frank, I never thought that a poustinia as a *vocation for life* would take root on this continent. This, frankly, at the time, was inconceivable as far as I was concerned, but as the bible says, "God's ways are not our ways."

One day a Trappist arrived on leave from his monastery looking for a place where he could try out the eremitical way of life that he had dreamed of for years. I showed him the shingled house in the hills in the midst of the forest and he took to it immediately. As we discussed the situation I explained to him that there was in Russia a type of people who, though accepting the vocation of a poustinik for life, had a different notion of solitude than the Western hermit. I explained to him the difference between the poustinik and the Western hermit. He was quite taken by that Russian style and so began spending three days in the poustinia in prayer and study (for he was a scripture scholar), and the remaining days teaching and serving the community.

But an amazing thing suddenly happened. Four more priests eventually came to embrace the full vocation of the Russian poustinik of three days in and four days out, and two women did likewise. For each we built a little log cabin, for theirs, by God's grace, is a life vocation.

One day I was praying in my own little poustinia and suddenly I was overwhelmed by the immensity of God's design for little Madonna House. Out of the memories that were in my heart and which he brought forth, he built the poustinias, for who else but God could do it? Not only did he bring forth and build them, not only did he bring people eager to fill them, not only did he make the poustinia a life vocation for Canada and America, but like the good seed thrown from the hands of the sower, this idea fell onto good soil and seemed to be spreading across the continent!

5

The Western Poustinik

What is the difference between the poustinias of Russia
that I have described in the earlier chapters and what is
happening here at Madonna House? The poustinik way
of life here is still in a stage of growth and evolution. I
will describe what is happening here, and also discuss some
Western notions such as "involvement" and "availability,"
which are understood differently in the Eastern mind.

Times have changed, and the ways of men have
changed. The world has become urbanized. But all the
more, then, is there need for solitude, for the silence of
God, away from the traffic and all the other noises. What
has *not* changed is God's grace to men.

I think there will be a renewal, with a different accent,
of people who want to embrace, perhaps for life, the vocation of a hermit. I think that there are going to be hermits
around our first farmhouse poustinia, though I do not know
what shape or form their life-styles will take.

The Trappist of whom I spoke earlier, and who eventually joined our community, spends Monday through Thurs-
day in his poustinia. As a scripture scholar he has a large
library. God knows that the world is in need of this teaching aspect of his priesthood and his knowledge. He has a

telephone, and he dictates a lot of letters. He translates books and writes papers. He is busy, and the world penetrates into his poustinia. It is a mixed kind of solitude, not the Russian type of poustinia in its fullness. Perhaps that's the way it should be; perhaps that's the way God wants it to be in these days of *aggiornamento*. Here I think we must wait and pray because God alone can define, slowly and realistically, this vocation that is evolving at Madonna House. At times, I must admit, I am confused about it; but I leave it all to God.

Another difference is in the area of fasting. Sometimes the poustiniks come to meals during their three days in solitude. Sometimes they fast for two or three days on bread, tea and/or coffee. Here again I have no judgment to make and no answers to give. I am just waiting to see what the Lord has in mind concerning our New World poustinias. Waiting is a long, confused, and painful time. But it is necessary now, and I feel I would be failing the members of the community if I did not wait. The translation of the real poustinia into the modern one will mean that God will lead us slowly toward the answers as to how and in what direction these poustinias will develop.

What is undeniable at the moment is that the poustinias at Madonna House have already helped many priests, sisters, and lay people to find their way to God, to know him better, to find the strength to do his will with greater love and fidelity. This is the fact, and every year we add more. There does not seem to be any end in sight.

In my own heart, the vision of the poustinia is twofold. I see people—perhaps even priests—coming to stay in the poustinia for maybe a year or more. On the other hand, I see the real poustinia in which the original idea of a man living in the desert as they did in Russia really happening here, because we need people who will stay in this silence of God and who are not distracted by a thousand noises within themselves and by demands made upon them—not entirely wrong demands, but not entirely right ones either. These silent ones—the ones that will really pray—will have all of humanity in their poustinias. They will do their own spiritual direction, write letters—and all this slowly, thoughtfully, in the secret silence between them and God. Maybe I am mistaken, yet I think there will be such persons. They will be spiritual directors from a distance. Directees will come and knock at their doors, so to speak.

I can foresee laymen and laywomen embracing this full hermit vocation, perhaps only coming down to Madonna House for Sunday Mass. They will remain in their poustinias the rest of the week. I would like to see them occupied with some manual craft—perhaps a little vegetable garden if possible. But this is secondary and unimportant. These people will be great lovers of solitude and of the silence of God.

Those who live such a permanent form of the poustinia will need more books than the bible, but I think they will have to spend at least a year with the bible. Others will tend to a more active-contemplative life; the world needs them as well. But I hope that there will be some who will be totally immersed in the silence of God and in prayer. I think there will be such. God will raise them up because the world so desperately needs them too.

You see how lost I am in speaking about this evolution of the poustinia! The poustinia ought to be the place where the noise of the soul is completely muted, where the intellect is muted also, and where this great listening to the silence of God takes place. I hope that the poustinikki of the modern world will be men and women of great poverty, that they will reduce their wardrobes to the bare essentials. Again, at this time, I don't want to lay down any rules. People at Madonna House will have to pray so as to direct each person to be the kind of poustinik that he or she must be.

The poustinia can never simply be a place of rest—sleeping, recreation, a "change of pace." The poustinia is a holy place, so holy that one trembles when one enters. It is not a place for dropping in for tea or coffee! It is not an eating place, nor a sleeping place. It is God's place, and the only person who can sleep or take full meals there is the poustinik or his pupil, or his co-poustinik. It should not be used for anything else. It breaks my heart when we have to use the poustinia buildings for anything else. Perhaps I am too sensitive in this regard.

Yes, more people will be coming to "make poustinia" and, yes, we will probably be building more of them. For the people who come to be in the poustinia for a day, two days, or longer, let them pray and fast as much as their health and age allow. If possible, let them have a hard bed; if they are infirm, a mattress will be permissible.

Let only the priests decide who is to go into the poustinia, for it is a priestly affair. Let the one who goes there be always truthful about his motives and not go there simply to have a good sleep or a day away from the tensions of life. Let them go there to enter the great silence of God, and to pray. If they enter for any other reason, however well distinguished or rationalized, the poustinia will not be a blessing upon them; it might be a curse. Nor can the poustinia become a place where everybody wants to go so they can say they have made a poustinia at Madonna House! That would be wrong. Let the priests pray much themselves so that they will be able to discern and make the decision as to just who should go into the poustinia.

Thus the phenomenon of the Western poustinia will slowly unfold itself. As the apostolate grows in wisdom and grace we might be sent people who really wish to live as close as possible to the Russian ideal. Then again, perhaps this ideal is gone. Perhaps these people will never return. Perhaps it will be a different kind of poustinia. It is too early to say. But I think that this hunger for the silence of God, this passivity of the silent soul, is going to come back. I believe there will be people to hear the word of God and who will take all of humanity into the poustinia with them. I believe there will be people who realize that it is this personal holocaust for humanity which can bring, with childlike simplicity, the words of God which they heard in the great silence back to the world.

These people are going to come because our age needs men of prayer, men of solitude, men who hunger to hear the voice of God directly, and who seek to know God by personal contact with him, and not through books alone. I think that there will be many poustinias opened across this North American land. Madonna House will have its share of the hungry ones who come to make this contact with God through the lifting of their arms in prayer and mortification. People will come to us who desire to contact the living God by emptying themselves of everything and by leaving everything at the threshold of the poustinia, so they can enter the poustinia empty in order to be filled with God. People will come who wish to hear God speak, to pass his word on to all they meet, and then return again to the silence of God.

I believe that God is even now raising up these men and women because there is so little silence of heart in the world. There is so much noise in the souls, minds, and hearts of men that God's voice cannot be heard. So he himself will call many to come and listen to his silence, to immerse themselves in it. Then he will send them forth to be prophets of today, to be his voice once again, across all the lands of the world. He will send them to a world that needs to hear his voice through the lips of its own brothers and sisters as it did of old when God sent the world his Son to speak. I personally do not know how to adapt from the old to the new. But God does.

Naturally, the form which the poustinia takes is dependent very much on notions of spirituality. Here I would like to discuss, above all, the notion of "involvement" as it is seen by Easterners and Westerners. The importance of this notion for the evolution of the poustinia is evident.

One day, back in February of 1971, I was asked by our three women poustinikki: "What is our involvement in Madonna House?" I answered that, first of all, involvement is the realization of our weakness. St. Paul says, "I glory in my weakness," and, "When I am weak, then I am strong." Let us go a bit deeper into this experience of weakness.

We are *anawim*, men who depend on God and know this as a fact. We are the poor of God who lean on him and know that without him we can do nothing. This is the kind of weakness I am talking about. When you are weak in that way, God becomes your strength. What is the poustinik's involvement in Madonna House? That you have time to realize who you are and to rejoice that you are saved sinners. The poustinik is a person who has time to ponder this every moment and to rejoice with a deep joy that he is totally dependent on God. If you are dependent on God, you can then call upon him for all your needs, and you know that God will listen.

The poustinik is a gardener tilling his fields, taking out all the weeds. He is harrowing so he can plow and get the roots out. Then God can sow there the seeds he wants. The poustinik is busy making the desert into a garden.

This gardening is the poustinik's basic kind of involvement. Such involvement is an opening to great risk. It is an opening to pain and to joy. It is both of these because it is an opening to Christ.

Westerners may see this as a strange kind of involvement. Strange because it seems to turn you inward toward yourself for a while, as if you took a broom to sweep yourself out under the guidance of God. Yes, you are involved in sweeping out the corridors of your mind and the corners of your heart, and all this is done in tremendous peace.

Another dimension of involvement in the community is the involvement of prayer. People will come to you and say, "Will you pray for me especially?" or "My sister has just had an operation," or similar things. People will ask for such individual things. I suggest you have an intention book, like I have, and when people ask, put that intention in your book. It will make you really take notice of the request. Perhaps you may have a little shelf under your icon where you can keep the book. (I do this. I have a silly idea that Our Lady reads it at night to her Son. That's a very childish idea—but I leave the book there just the same!)

When people ask you to pray for them you should feel some real kind of responsibility to do so. I often mention the petitions audibly in prayer, or at Mass, or sometimes I write a note to one of the priests and ask them to pray for such and such. Of course, sometimes I forget and I say, "Look Lord, help the people who asked me to pray for them yesterday," or whenever they asked. I'm never scrupulous about it; that would be foolish. But this is another way you are involved in the community.

Westerners in a poustinia may feel guilty because they are not "part of the community." Such a question would never enter my mind. If a Russian built a poustinia next to the village, he automatically knows that he is part of that village. He doesn't have to be told that he is now part of the community. Being part of the community is not a matter of geography. If your spiritual director says that you should spend three days in the poustinia, you spend three days. If he thinks you should spend four, you spend four. If he thinks you should come out of the poustinia for a while altogether, you come out. *Wherever you are in obedience, you are part of the community*. It is not a matter of being inside or outside the poustinia.

One of the main causes of this feeling of guilt for being "separated from the community" stems, I think, from the Western notion of production. The West values itself for its ability to produce things. Priests, nuns and lay people tend to evaluate themselves interiorly by what they can *produce*. Priests especially do not realize that their presence is enough. I often tell priests who work in parishes that one of the best things they can "do" is simply walk around their neighborhoods and be present to their people. If they don't do something, they feel that they are wasting their lives away. So it is with the poustinik. There is an inability to realize that the presence of a person who is in love with God is enough, and that nothing else is needed. That doesn't mean that the poustinik's assistance in definite ways cannot be helpful to the community. But it does mean that one should be perfectly at peace even (should I say especially?) when one hasn't got "something to do."

Now for the poustinik, this is exceedingly difficult. A

priest poustinik, for example, should be totally indifferent as to how many directees he has. It should be the same for a nonpoustinik, but especially for a poustinik, he doesn't go out to "get directees." People may be drawn to this poustinik or to that one, and they may come to talk with him. The poustinik, however, ought to be totally indifferent as to how many directees he has, or who comes to visit him. He does not reach out and say to people, "Oh, come and see me sometime." The door is unlatched, but you do not select people to come and open it!

Let us say that somebody is talking to you on the days when you are out, and the thought comes to you, "Perhaps I should invite this person to my poustinia where we could talk better." No, don't do that, unless the person asks. The request must come from the other. The poustinik doesn't ask them. He is peaceful. He answers questions but he doesn't invite people to his poustinia. Your spiritual director or someone in authority may ask you to show them your poustinia. That's a different question. But the poustinik doesn't reach out to people to take them to the poustinia. You open your heart to receive what comes from God.

This attitude must be one of the most excruciating things for a Westerner, to be, in a sense, so seemingly passive. It is not so easy to be sensitive to the delicate action of the Spirit in this way. The Spirit moves so very lightly, lighter than the breeze, lighter than the air. When you breathe you are not aware of the air in the room. You are so used to breathing that you don't think about the air. The poustinik must become conscious of the air.

A poustinik is detached from all things—even holy things. Because it's "holy" to have directees, because it's "holy" to have people come and talk, it's all the more difficult to be detached from them. It's hard to just stand there or to be there in the poustinia like an idiot, not "doing" anything. Well, that's something of what the Lord said to St. Francis of Assisi: "I want you to be a fool the likes of whom have never been seen before." For a modern man or woman to just stand there and be Jesus' kind of idiot is very hard.

Years ago, when one of our priests first came, he asked, after a couple of weeks, "Catherine, what kind of contribution shall I make?" I said, "Your presence, Father." He brushed that aside for the third time and said, "Yes, I know that, but what *other contribution* can I make?" Well, it took a long time for him who had been a superior of a school to understand that the contribution was himself. And it was difficult. He was very happy when he finally got some definite assignment. I understand now how difficult this must have been for him, this acceptance of simple presence as one's contribution.

I think that this is what God calls the poustinik to: a total purgation, a total self-emptying. In the gospel of the Passion we see how Christ is silent before the authorities. Imagine, God is silent! He asks for nothing, and he gives himself. If you want to see what a "contribution" really is, look at the Man on the cross. That's a contribution. When you are hanging on a cross you can't do anything because you are crucified. That is the essence of a poustinik. That is his or her contribution. The poustinik's loneliness is of salvific and cosmic proportions. This is his contribution. He must deeply meditate on this because the notion is very profound. By hanging on his cross of loneliness, his healing rays, like the rays of the sun, will penetrate the earth.

The poustinik stays in his poustinia and conquers his

desire to contribute in his way; that is, the way *he feels* he ought to be contributing. Little by little he agrees to an interior stripping, to becoming naked before the Lord. Just as the rays of the sun are healing, and nobody can say for sure exactly how far they penetrate into the universe, so no one can tell how far the loneliness of a poustinik united with God penetrates into the world. The world is cold. Someone must be on fire so that people can come and put their cold hands and feet against that fire. If anyone allows this to happen, but especially the poustinikki, then he will become a fireplace at which men can warm themselves. His rays will go out to the ends of the earth.

The English word "zeal" usually means intensity of action. A person is zealous about his farming or some crusade. But real zeal is standing still and letting God be a bonfire in you. It's not very easy to have God's fire within you. Only if you are possessed of true zeal will you be able to contain God's bonfire. We must allow God to "contribute" through us, which means that nakedness before him must come first.

Young people use the word "vibes" these days. People emit "good vibes" and "bad vibes." Well, "vibes" will eventually bring people to the poustinik, because people can feel spirituality. To speak very colloquially, a poustinik is one who allows the "vibes of the Lord" to draw people to the poustinia. Such is real involvement.

6

Approaching the Poustinia

Many people come to Madonna House who have never before heard of the poustinia. The members of the community often tell me that these people get nervous and jittery about going into a poustinia for their one day. In this chapter I imagine myself talking rather informally to all those people who in the future may be drawn to go into the poustinia for the first time. In a sort of "schmazz" state of mind you may be wondering: "Where do I go? What do I do? What do I take with me?" If I could talk to each of these people beforehand I would say something such as the following:

Relax! You have heard the word poustinia and it sounds like a mysterious Russian deal of some sort. There's nothing mysterious about it! A poustinia is just an ordinary log cabin with a wood stove, a table and chair, and a bed. You will find there a bible, and a little outline* I wrote which tells you what to do more or less—because I can't really tell you what to do. Nobody can tell you what to do. You are about to have a rendezvous, a date with Christ. For 24 hours you are going to be alone with God and the only book that you are going to read is the bible. Don't take

---

*Cf. pp. 54-55.

any others! If you want to sleep, sleep. If you want to walk, walk. It's up to you. Once you enter the poustinia you do what the Spirit tells you to do. There's nothing frightening about it.

Sometimes we are so exhausted mentally, morally and physically that we just can't do much of anything. Going into the poustinia we just flop down! Well, to sleep in the arms of Christ is a pretty good idea. You don't have to do anything. It's being simple in your relationship with God. I often make believe (for I am full of imagination) that I say to the Lord, "Lord, have a cup of coffee with me." So I imagine God is there and we have a cup of coffee and I chew the fat with him. Why not?

Once, on the first day of a poustinia, I slept a great deal, I was so exhausted. I couldn't even read the bible. So I said to the Lord, "OK, now you've given me the gift of sleep, give me some good dreams too." I had lovely dreams and the next day I prayed. I was refreshed. I was able to be attentive. You see, there is a kind of art to relaxation. With God you don't have to put on your best bib and tucker. You can just be yourself. Remember, he knows all about you, from A to Z, from the nails of your toes to the hair of your head. To try to fool the Lord by putting on any kind of show is absolutely idiotic. The poustinia is one place where you can relax a little as if you were a piece of pancake dough. He knows all about you. Have a little chat with him, snooze a little, do a little reading, go out and look at the grass and say, "Gee, how beautiful you made the grass," or "How beautiful you made the snow," whichever it is, or "How lovely the rain is." That's the sort of thing you can do. There's nothing frightening about it.

The one who goes to the poustinia for the first time,

for a day or two, will experience a certain amount of interior noise. The first time one of the staff went she said to me on returning, "Boy, that was a terrible experience! You know what happened to me?" I said, "Yes, I think I do. But tell me anyway." She said, "All my thoughts buzzed in me like flies. I was thinking that my jeans needed patching, that the garden needed weeding. I thought about everything except God." I said, "Oh, that's perfectly natural." It takes a long time for modern man to close the wings of his intellect and to open the door of his heart.

For those of you who go into the poustinia for a day or two, this is the essence of it: to fold the wings of your intellect. In this civilization of the West everything is sifted through your heads. You are so intellectual, so full of knowledge of all kinds. The poustinia brings you into contact first and foremost with solitude. Secondly, it brings you in contact with God. Even if you don't feel anything at all, the fact remains that you have come to have a date with God, a very special rendezvous. You have said to the Lord, "Lord, I want to take this 24, 36, 48 hours out of my busy life and I want to come to you because I am very tired. The world is not the way you want it, and neither am I. I want to come and rest on your breast as St. John the Beloved. That's why I have come to this place." Or you might say, "Lord, I don't believe in you. I just don't think you exist. I think you are dead. But they tell me that in this strange little cabin in the midst of the woods you might be alive. I want to come in and see. May I?" There are a thousand reasons why a person might come to a retreat like this, but the essence is the folding of that intellect that makes so many towers of Babel and is still doing it—and opening the heart that alone can receive the word of God.

St. Paul says, "Pray without ceasing." Prayer is the source and the most intimate part of our lives. "When you pray, go into your room, close the door, and pray to your Father in secret." These words of Our Lord mean that you must enter into yourself and make a sanctuary there; the secret place is the human heart. The life of prayer—its intensity, its depth, its rhythm—is the measure of our spiritual health and reveals us to ourselves. "Rising long before daybreak, he went out and departed into a desert place, and there he prayed." With the ascetics, the desert is interiorized, and signifies the concentration of a recollected spirit. At this level, where man knows how to be silent, true prayer is found. Here he is mysteriously visited.

This is another thing that the poustinia will teach you if you allow it to do so. It will teach you prayer, a different prayer than perhaps you have been used to.

Often people say that they have no time for prayer. Where is the place for prayer? Prayer is inside. I am a church. I am a temple of the Father, the Son, and the Holy Spirit. They came to me. The Lord said that he and his Father would come and make their dwelling with me. I don't have to go anywhere. Neither does this mean that you shouldn't render glory to God in church where everybody else comes to pray, but it means that you should pray constantly. There should be no break in our prayer. There is a poustinia of the heart. Why should my heart be removed from God while I am talking to you? When you are in love with someone, it seems that the face of the beloved is before you when you drive, when you type, when you are taking out insurance, and so on. Somehow or other we can encompass these two realities, the face of the beloved and whatever we happen to be doing.

My friends, prayer is like that. If you fall in love then it's impossible to separate life and breath from prayer. Prayer is simply union with God. Prayer does not need words. When people are in love they look at each other, look into each other's eyes, or a wife simply lies in the arms of her husband. Neither of them talks. When love reaches its apex it cannot be expressed anymore. It reaches that immense realm of silence where it pulsates and reaches proportions unknown to those who haven't entered into it. Such is the life of prayer with God. You enter into God and God enters into you, and the union is constant.

The day I was baptized my little feet made the first step toward that union with God for which I was born. I can walk through my life and never remember. Such will be an arid life. It will be an unhappy life. But no matter what happens to me, if I remember that I exist to be united with God, and that I am united with God every minute, all I have to do is think about it. In fact, I don't even have to think. His face is always before me.

This is what the icon expresses—the face of God. The icon, whether of Our Lord or of Our Lady, is simply a corridor through which I go. As my life goes on slowly, the veil that separates me from God is rent, and I begin to see the outlines and features of the Lord that will be fully revealed to me when I die.

Now I hope you are not going to be frightened anymore when you set out to go to the poustinia. I hope you will be in possession of your soul, and not run around looking for what, when, how, and so on. It's no use going into the poustinia when you are all whsssssst! The day before the poustinia, calm your mind. Close your intellect. Open your heart. Smile at everybody—especially at yourself—and be at peace. Say to the person taking care of you, "I am at peace. Whenever you are ready to take me, I will be here."

My mother used to go to one of the poustinikki for spiritual direction. He was an old man. I remember walking ten miles one way to visit him. When you first enter a poustinia you are supposed to look at the icon. There is an icon in every poustinia. You bow before it. This is to acknowledge that the head of this humble place is Our Lord, or Our Lady, depending on whose icon it is. Then you say, "Peace to this house," and the person answers, "Peace to you also," or something similar.

So this is how you should approach the poustinia, unfrightened, in great peace, looking forward to your rendezvous with the Lord. If I were to draw up a little list for you as a kind of road map for your first trip to the poustinia, it would look something like this:

1. The poustinia is a place where you are going to meet Christ in joyful solitude.
2. There is nothing to be afraid of, for Christ is perfect love and perfect love casts out all fears.
3. The poustinia is a prayer house which you enter to be alone with God, for the length of time approved by your spiritual director.
4. You don't take any books with you because the only book that should be read in the poustinia is the bible; it is there waiting for you.
5. The poustinia is a place not only of a rendezvous with Christ, not only a time for solitude and silence, but also a time of penance, for when you lift your heart to the Lord in prayer you should, in a manner of speaking, lift both spiritual arms of penance and prayer, like Moses on the mountain.
7. When you go to the poustinia we give you a loaf of

bread for each day you are staying. Also a thermos of hot water to make tea.

8. Don't get excited about it!

9. Above all, be at peace, because you enter into a visit with Christ, into his solitude, peacefully. Set your soul in patience, waiting for the person who is taking you to the poustinia.

10. Please pray for us while you are there.

7

Poustinia in the Marketplace

It happened during the visitation of one of our houses in 1968. It seemed to me that the members of our staff there were growing as individuals, that they were beginning to understand the price involved in forming a community of love. All three were drawn to prayer and were standing still before God. But nevertheless, with all these graces, there was a sense of frustration, a lack of direction as to just where the *house* was going. They could not see their role clearly. The whole atmosphere in which they worked seemed amorphous, its contours constantly changing. There was a tiredness present, but at the same time a sort of expectation. There was patience and hope in each of them.

One morning, as I was listening with my heart to the various reports being given, I was suddenly shaken by a thought that had never even dimly entered my mind or soul. I saw three people who perhaps were being called to be a *poustinia in the marketplace!* And so, at one point in the meeting, after the reports had been given, there was a heavy silence. Into that silence a bombshell fell! Quite unexpectedly, and almost without knowing what I was saying, I put the following question to everyone: "What if the Lord means this house to be a poustinia in the marketplace?"

I must admit that besides startling everyone else, I

startled myself. At no previous time had I thought of such a thing. Yet, there it was, a bolt of fire, unexpected, burning brightly in the hand of God. I must admit that it was an extraordinary experience for me and for all those present. A Pentecostal experience. Not one of us doubted that it was from the Holy Spirit. It came like a wind, like a tongue of fire. There was no negative reaction. Though shaken, our silence had the quality of awe, astonishment, fear, some bewilderment. Yet our hearts listened. In some strange way we knew that this was the answer.

Then we began discussing the details a little bit. What does it mean? Where will it lead? What changes will it entail, if any?

The answers came slowly, painfully, but clearly. It would mean a deepening of relationships with one another. They would be called to form among themselves a very deep community of love. They would become, as it were, the strength, the hidden help, the arrow pointing to God constantly, the hidden powerful help for all the rest of Madonna House apostolate. Among themselves a new and awesome openness would have to exist. Fear of revealing their weaknesses to one another would eventually have to be overcome. They would have to stand naked before one another, for they were called to follow the naked Christ.

Nothing would change, and everything would change. They would continue to be engaged in mazes of meetings, contacts, plunging ever deeper into the secular society. They would remain on the important but humdrum level of this strange apostolate of martyrdom and patience, dealing with migrant leagues, open housing, model cities, and the rest.

But everything would be changed in depth. Living in the poustinia of their house would mean three people standing still before God in order to walk better with men. The door of their hearts, as the door of their home, must never be closed henceforth. Their pilgrimage to the Absolute, though hidden from the eyes of men, would be the same one that Our Lord had entrusted to his apostles and disciples. They would have to accept what it means to be an apostolate and at the same time a poustinia. They would be a hermitage in the midst of the marketplace that witnesses to that part of our Little Mandate: "Go into the marketplace and stay with me. Be a light to your neighbor's feet. Go without fear into the depth of men's hearts. I shall be with you. Pray always. I shall be your rest." They will be infiltrators of Christ into the marketplace.

Another question loomed very large: What would be the face of this apostolate? The answer was both simple and very complex. Slowly, at the price of constant prayer, openness to one another, surrender to their vocation, *the face of the apostolate would be to daily reveal more and more the face of Christ.* As they enter the abysses and precipices of this new accent of their vocation, they would enter more deeply into the heights and depths of Christ's plan and life. Thereby, in deed and in truth, in some fantastic way, they would "make up what is wanting in the sufferings of Christ" (Col 1:24).

Yes, to me the face of their apostolate was strikingly and awesomely clear. It shook me to the very depth of my soul. I could not believe, sinner that I am, that the Lord was smiling at me. For here, 38 years later, in another country, he was telling me that my original call was right. I had had to be patient, waiting for it to be incarnated, so that I might grow in faith, hope and love.

For the face of this apostolate, this poustinia in the marketplace, was exactly what I thought had been my original call and dream in the Lord when I went into Portland Street in the city of Toronto. I went there to live forever (or so I thought) in this modern Nazareth—but the Lord decreed otherwise. Yet now, 38 years later, he was asking a group of spiritual children, his and mine, to become a Nazareth in the marketplace. I saw that that dream was to be the face of this apostolate.

Yes, the face of this apostolate would be Nazareth! Nazareth, where he spent his hidden life. Nazareth, where the days were humdrum and ordinary, where no visible results were forthcoming except tables and chairs. Nazareth, where the Son of God was simply the son of Mary and Joseph to all the people around him. Nazareth, where he lived as we will have to live, in the company of Mary and Joseph, and from them learn the silence of the heart. Nazareth, the preparation of his entrance into the desert, which was already a kind of desert, situated in a small village of Galilee.

This house would now have to take on the face of Nazareth. It would continue to intensify its very ordinariness and simplicity, bearing with people who will not understand why they are *producing so little*. They will have to accept the fact that people will say of them what others said of Jesus, "Can anything good come out of Nazareth?" But slowly, very slowly, according to the leadings of the Holy Spirit, people whom they never suspected they could reach will gather around them. Through their prayerful, hidden, and seemingly unproductive life, God will prepare them for new contacts and new works according to *his* plan and not *theirs*.

It is not enough for only one person in a house to understand this notion of the poustinia in the marketplace. It is necessary for the whole community to understand it. Slowly, humbly, fully aware of the pain, all must understand the difficulties, the kenosis, the selflessness that Christ desires from all who enter this desert in the marketplace. It is necessary that all the members of the community understand that, especially in the first year or so, and perhaps for many years to come, Satan is going to buffet them and tempt them as he did Christ in the desert.

These temptations will not be the ordinary ones to commit fornication or to be greedy. In a sense, these temptations are past, though we must never forget our humanity; in some form or other they will be with us because we are sinners.

But more subtle temptations will come. The devil will try to twist the meaning of their vocation. He will suggest how impossible it is to form a community of love, especially for people of our age who are so wounded and suffering from neuroses of all kinds. The devil will concentrate on this because the essence of a house becoming a poustinia in the marketplace will be that its members really bear with one another, and cover themselves with humility, compassion, and love toward one another. Yes, the devil will attack especially this admonition of St. Paul's to "bear with one another." He will attack it with all sorts of "logical" arguments and prove that it is *just not possible*.

The next temptation will be to complacency and mediocrity. They will be tempted to settle down because now they have really achieved "good interpersonal relationships." Everything is now "nice and smooth."

*   *   *   *   *   *   *

Time passed. There was a certain amount of confusion in the minds of many people as to just what this poustinia

in the marketplace really was. I realized that in the excitement of that first Pentecostal moment during the visitation, I might not have spelled out exactly what this new
aspect of the apostolate should be. During the months
which followed, the idea grew and developed in my own
mind. I wrote back several times to the house we had
visited, trying to clarify the concept for them.

"Your poustinia in the marketplace begins with prayer,
much prayer. It does not mean that you are not doing the
work you have been doing: housing, migrant workers, and
so on. No. You must understand that the poustinia *begins
in your heart.* It is not a place, a geographical spot. It is
not first and foremost a house or a room. It is within your
heart. It is implementing the prayer of St. Francis. That
is the work of the poustinik in the marketplace, to be hidden
as Christ was hidden in Nazareth.

"When this work of the Holy Spirit is really allowed
to take place in a human heart, the person is utterly indifferent as to where, geographically, he is situated. It is
possible to live in a lovely little house while inwardly,
spiritually, you are clad like John the Baptist in animal
skins and eating locusts and wild honey. Even there you
can fast from your illusory needs and begin in deed and in
truth to preach the gospel with every step you take, with
every word you say. You can concentrate on forming a
community of love among yourselves.

"If this inner poustinia, this stripping of oneself, this
kenosis, is begun, it means that you kneel before the Lord
and say, 'Here I am, Lord, do with me as you will. Speak,
for your servant is listening. Lord, I thank you for all you
have given me, for all you have taken away from me, for
all you have left me.' When you have done that you will
have begun to understand the poustinia in the marketplace.

"All of this can only be achieved by prayer, and the greatest prayer is the Eucharist. Times spent before the Blessed Sacrament and in chapel form part of this prayer. Of course, prayer is much broader than all these. Prayer is as infinite as God. Prayer is constant. Prayer is work. Prayer is loving. Prayer is dying. Prayer is stripping oneself of one's needs. Prayer is serving the needs of others. Prayer is conversation with God that never ceases. Prayer is life in Nazareth, and doing the work of Our Lady, or helping St. Joseph in the carpentry shop. Prayer is living in the presence of God.

"If you have this poustinia in your heart, your likes and dislikes will disappear. With joy you will go to meetings, but now you will know that you bring into those meetings not so much your own wisdom, your own talents, your own know-how, but that you are bringing the Lord. Your presence at those meetings will become a *mysterium*, a mystery of the Lord's presence.

"In this way the poustinia will begin to bear fruit. You will bring to the secular society in which you live Love, who is a Person, who is God. Now your work and your prayer blend into preaching the gospel of love by just being where you are and where God wants you to be at this given moment. In other words, you are doing the will of God and bringing him in hidden and mysterious ways to all those around you who might not even know his name. As the days roll on, your lives will become flames.

"In the book *The Struggle With God* a strange anecdote is related:

> A young man once went to an old
> ascetic to be instructed in the
> way of perfection by the old man,
> but the old man did not say a word.

The other asked him the reason for
his silence. "Am I then a superior
to command you?" he answered. "I
shall say nothing. Do if you want,
what you see me do."*

"This is how you must act yourselves. Because we
belong to an apostolate, we are tabbed, catalogued. When
we come to a meeting people expect us to have some special
knowledge and experience. True, we may have a little
more knowledge and experience, but as far as you are concerned, most of the time, you will be there silently, like
that old ascetic, and your silence will teach.

"You see that the poustinia in the marketplace is not
for amateurs! You must have a very good schedule of work,
and by work I mean whatever God demands of you at a
given moment. The will of God for you, as for all our
missions, is *contact with people*. It is unimportant what
form this contact takes—meetings, discussion groups, and
so on. The modern expression for this is 'interpersonal relationships.' (Frankly, what is often *called* interpersonal
relationships is a lot of nonsense!) Interpersonal relationships in the Christian sense means loving contact, bringing
the mystery of God's presence in you to others.

"That is what I mean by a poustinia in the marketplace.
It is a mystery of God's love in which he asks you to be
present where often his presence is not experienced. Yours
is an apostolate of bringing the Christ who dwells in you to
meeting after meeting. If the occasion demands it, you
speak of course on whatever topic is up for consideration.
But the real reason for your attendance is so that by your
physical presence—*by your being there*—you make Christ

*Paul Evdokimov, Paulist Press (Glen Rock, New Jersey), p. 128.

more present. You witness first of all by your presence.

"As you know only too well, the divisions, arguments, and power plays that take place at meetings witness to the fragmentation of humanity. By your presence in love, you have to witness to how much time is wasted, how much selfishness is going on, how much greed there is for power, attention, and recognition.

"At these meetings you see a microscopic picture of the splintered world. Then you return to your house, and by forming a community of love among yourselves, you help to heal the divisions which were present at the meetings. By your recollection, by your quiet hearts, by your recitation of the Jesus Prayer, by your Masses, and especially by your peaceful lives, you enter into the mystery of God's healing. You help to heal the man besieged by robbers along the road. He is a symbol, of course, of all the people at these meetings who are so desperately searching for truth, for answers, for God. If by prayer you have received food from God, you should be able, at these meetings, to give the oil of tenderness and the wine of compassion, first to each other, and then to everyone you meet. All this is done silently, in the secret places of your hearts.

"An incident from the life of Dorothy Day expresses well what I am trying to say here. Dorothy went to Rome during the Council. Several years later when I met her in Rome I asked her what she did during the time the Council was in session. She said she had simply taken a room in a poor quarter of the city, and for ten days she fasted on bread and water and prayed for the Council. That was all she did! Then she returned to New York the way she had come—on a freight boat! Maybe this was the reason why the Council was so successful. In the eyes of God, who knows?

"I realize that you are still unsure of your 'role.' I am

not particularly fond of the word 'role'—'goal' would be better. Your goal had already been defined for you when you were baptized, and it is clear: union with God. It begins now, and ends in the beatific vision. It is reached by a thousand little goals, daily ones, and can be achieved only by tearing masks away, one after the other, and by having one's heart opened by the lance of love.

"To reach the beatific vision you must reach union with each other. In forming a family, a community of love, you have to accept the cross—embrace it gloriously and willingly. Your cross is composed of little things, and of the acceptance of each other as you are. You must develop the ability to see the positive in each other, to see each other's beauty, to see each other's talents, and to rejoice in them and be glad about them.

"As you grow in love, you help each other, gently, peacefully, constantly, accepting the weaknesses of each other with deep love, with great patience; for that is how the Lord has treated you. Yes, your first goal which alone will lead you to your final goal will be to establish a family, a 'community of love,' accepting all the pain, the problems, the difficulties that every family must go through if it is going to become a community of love.

"As you know, I attended the International Lay Congress in Rome. One of the most outstanding experiences was the confrontation of the underdeveloped countries with the West. It was the African, Indian, Pakistani representatives who point-blank asked the theological experts of the West the following questions.

"A simple little farm woman from Cameroon, who represented two thousand mothers, asked: 'We, the ordinary folk of Cameroon, Africa, have tried to bring up our children in the love of God and neighbor. True, we were poor. You realized that you had kept us poor by your colonialism. Then we thought that you had had a change of heart. You offered us scholarships to Catholic institutions in Europe, Canada, and America. With joy we sent our sons and daughters to you. But now we weep, because you have given them such secular knowledge that they have returned without faith, and with hate in their hearts. Now they are desirous of getting rid of you because you gave them knowledge but no love.'

"A Vietnamese, thin and gaunt, said: 'I have been sent by my people to represent Catholic families. How can you believe in the Prince of Peace while you continue to wage war?' A Hindu asked: 'I have been listening for five days now to discussions on the Dutch liturgy, the Dutch catechism, on new theological approaches to this and that. But I have heard nothing about Jesus Christ, nothing about the need for contemplation and prayer. Why do you send us missionaries who are interested in so many things but do not show us the face of Christ?'

"To achieve this kind of missionary activity, we must follow Christ in the rhythm of his own life, the rhythm of solitude and action. What is needed today is to retire to solitude and silence, to hear the voice of God, to glorify and pray to him, and then to return to the secular world. Tragically, the West keeps brushing this aside and saying, 'Yes, these are the basic verities—but let's get down to action!'

"By the grace of the Holy Spirit, this is what Madonna House has been preaching all these years, and now I know why we have these poustinias. I implore you, dearly beloved, to meditate on what these poor nations have said in Rome. It applies directly to the poustinia in the marketplace.

"I know the price of making a family out of human beings, both a blood family and a spiritual family. The price is high, but so was the price that Christ paid for us. We have to be like seeds in his hands, cast out to the four winds by the Spirit into the soil he has chosen. The harvest he desires is primarily unity among yourselves. Then strangers will come and cease to be strangers, because your family, your community of love, will encompass them and heal them after it has healed you.

"Your notion of the poustinia in the marketplace is confused because of your overliteral, rational, compartmentalized Western mentality! You have an image in your minds of our original poustinia secluded in the woods. So you ask, 'What is this poustinia in the marketplace? Are we supposed to be hermits and recluses? How does it fit in with the action mandated by our apostolate?' Here I implore the grace and goodness of the Holy Spirit to give me word-images that might open up your vision of this extraordinary and beautiful vocation.

"Suppose that you were married and became pregnant. Would you stop cooking for your husband? Would you stop doing the laundry, the cleaning, stop going to meetings on racial justice and school affairs? No. You'd go about your daily business. The only difference between you and everyone else would be that you were carrying a child.

"Your womb is a poustinia for the child, and you carry him wherever you go. Wherever you go you are pregnant with Christ, and you bring his presence as you would bring the presence of a natural child. For when a woman is with child, people give her special attention. They smile, they offer her a comfortable place to sit down. She is a witness to life. She carries life around with her.

"Applying this example to the mystery of being pregnant

with God (and it applies to both men and women), you have, as it were, a *poustinia within you*. It is as if within you there was a little log cabin in which you and Christ were very close; in this attitude you go about your business. God forbid that you should all become recluses or hermits! That is not what is meant by being a poustinik in the marketplace. It means that within yourselves you have made a room, a log cabin, a secluded space. You have built it by prayer— the Jesus Prayer or whatever prayer you have found profitable. You should be more aware of God than anyone else, because you are carrying within you this utterly quiet and silent chamber. Because you are more aware of God, because you have been called to listen to him in your inner silence, you can bring him to the street, the party, the meeting, in a very special and powerful way. The power is his, but you have contributed your *fiat*. He has asked you and chosen you to be the carrier of that silent poustinia within yourself.

"In a manner of speaking, nothing has changed in your daily schedule. You are not 'retiring recluses.' Far from it! The new accent of your Madonna House vocation is to carry this poustinia into the marketplace. So you attend all the meetings as before, knowing in deep faith and its accompanying darkness that you are bringing Christ, the Christ who prayed to his Father all night, alone on the mountain. You bring the Christ who stole away from the crowds to pray. You are now carrying him back to the crowds. So you should be *with* the crowds.

"How to achieve this balance? How to achieve this ideal of being a poustinia in the marketplace both as a community and as an individual? The answer is simple: you pray more. You pray to the Holy Spirit to make your Eucharists more profound. You are constantly more attuned to God. You are more open with each other, and you talk about the Lord to each other.

"I don't know if I have succeeded in giving you a clearer idea of what this kind of poustinia of the marketplace is. It is not a matter of retiring to any basement! You live in the marketplace and carry the poustinia within you. That is your vocation. You are pregnant with Christ. You are Christ-bearers. You are poustinia bearers. Where? In the marketplace. To whom? To anyone whom you meet there, but especially to those you are mandated to be with. This eliminates, I hope, all notions of being recluses, of withdrawing from the marketplace."

* * * * * * *

One of my favorite sentences from Paul Claudel clarifies a bit more in depth, I think, the notion of the poustinia in the marketplace. He writes: "The Word is the adopted son of silence, for St. Joseph passes through the pages of the gospel without uttering a single word." Isn't that a beautiful sentence to meditate on for the rest of one's life?

There are also some passages in the book quoted before, *The Struggle With God,* which seem to me to be also relevant to this topic. He writes:

> To hear the voice of the Word, we
> must know how to listen to his silence,
> and *above all, to learn it ourselves.*
> Speaking from experience, the spiritual
> masters are very definite: "If one does
> not know how to give a place in his life
> to recollection and silence, it is im-
> possible for him to arrive at a higher
> degree and to be able to pray in public
> places" (p.177).

This is exactly what we have been talking about. This is

the poustinia in the marketplace. But listen to what follows: "This degree makes us aware that one part of us, being immersed in what is immediate, is always worried and distracted, while the other part observes this with astonishment and compassion." This ability to observe oneself with both astonishment and compassion is rare, but it comes if we allow a desert to develop in our hearts.

Then we proceed to the real essence of this whole matter·

> Recollection opens our soul to heaven,
> *but also to other men.* The contemplative life or the active life—
> this problem is somewhat artificial, says
> St. Serapion. The real problem is *that
> of the heart's dimension.* Acquire interior peace and a multitude of men will
> find their salvation near you. (*Ibid.*)

This is an interesting statement. The Saint does not say "through" you but "near" you. There is much to reflect on here.

St. Theresa used to say that to pray is to treat God like a friend. The essence of prayer is to hear the voice of another, of Christ, but likewise to hear the voice of each person I meet in whom Christ also addresses me. His voice comes to me in every human voice, and his face is infinitely varied. It is present in the face of the wayfarer on the road to Emmaus; it is present in the gardener speaking to Mary Magdalen, it is present in my next-door neighbor. God became incarnate so that man might contemplate his face in every face. Perfect prayer seeks this presence of Christ and recognizes it in every human face. The unique image of Christ is the icon, but every human face is an icon of Christ, discovered by a prayerful person.

The contemplative and active life cannot be separated.

This is so difficult for the West to understand. Its Roman, juridical attitude tends to label and classify and categorize everything. The active and contemplative life of the Christian is one life. This truth, plus the remarks about prayer, and everything else I have been discussing in this chapter, are in the realm of mystery and faith. They cannot be comprehended by the mind alone. They must be contemplated in the luminous darkness of faith. I hope this has all helped to clarify somewhat what this poustinia in the marketplace is all about.

Yes, I have tried to convey something of that strange spiritual experience that shook us all during that house visitation. If I used words like incredible, mystical, spiritual, awesome, incomprehensible, I haven't said anything, really. It was all so beyond words, yet it spoke to our hearts. The poustinia in the marketplace was born that day in the hearts of three women on a little street in a little house. Everyone of the Madonna House apostolate everywhere must have felt strangely blessed and must have rejoiced that the Lord in his infinite mercy extended our first poustinia right out into the marketplace. We of Madonna House ought to take off our shoes and walk softly because the things that are happening to us through the will of the Lord are beyond our understanding, and call for a faith that moves mountains.

There is a kind of flowering of the gospel taking place in our apostolate. We are coming to a new crossroads, and the arrow is pointing very clearly to one road. We don't have to stand for very long and wonder which road to take. The Lord is calling us *to stand still before him while walking with men.* Yes, the next step of our apostolate is the ability to walk with men and be contemplatives while we are walking.

Part II

Talks to
Poustinikki

8

Basic Spirituality

For the past few months now I have been getting together almost weekly with the poustinikki here at Madonna House. I have been trying to share, in an informal way, some aspects of the spirituality of the poustinia, and I would like to share some of them with you.

The poustinik lives very closely with the Blessed Trinity: Father, Son, and Holy Spirit. He should witness to the Trinity. When someone comes to the poustinia he should say, "Peace be with you," and the poustinik answers, "May the peace of the Father, the Son, and the Holy Spirit overshadow you." When a poustinik comes to a priest, and especially to his or her spiritual director, the poustinik says, "Bless me, Father, in the name of the Holy Trinity." Constant awareness of the Trinity engenders an ability to consider the Incarnation and thus to incarnate in one's life the Incarnation. The poustinik is plunged in the Trinity. Whenever you say the word "God," your heart must move toward the Trinity.

The Trinity moves, for God is eternally creative, and creation is expressed in movement. God is light, and you come to realize that you are being drawn by the Trinity into the light and into the movement of the Eternal Family.

You begin to know with a knowledge that you could never acquire by reading a million books. As you touch the Trinity you realize that God is love—and you know this with a knowledge that no one can take from you.

One enters the poustinia with an absolute simplicity, the simplicity of a little child, and there are no gimmicks of any kind. There is no, what you call, protocol. There is no horarium. There are none of these things. The poustinia is timeless. You must come to understand that you came from eternity and you will return to eternity. Especially those who live in the poustinia permanently, they live in timelessness. He who lives in timelessness lives in eternity, and he who lives in eternity is in touch with God, because that's what eternity is all about.

So you enter into the poustinia with a simple heart, knowing that you come from eternity, that from all eternity you were in the mind of God, and that you are *in it now*. With this simplicity comes a tremendous peace, a peace which shatters the division between life and death. The great fear of death gradually disappears, and that is the ultimate of simplicity, the simplicity of a child.

A child approaches death with perfect joy. I remember a child of about four or five years who was brought to view the body of his grandmother. He sort of waltzed up to the coffin, kissed his grandmother, patted her on the head, and said, "Oh, you're so cold. Don't worry, soon you'll be very, very warm. Everything is going to be warm." Somebody asked him (this was in Russia) why he said such a thing. "Oh," he said, "my mother told me that Grandma was going to Jesus. It's very cold on the way but warm when you get there." Now that's the simplicity of a child.

The poustinik should have a gentle attitude toward himself, toward other people, and toward all of God's creation. In other words, the attitude of the poustinik is a cosmic tenderness, a tenderness toward all God's creatures. But that tenderness and gentleness begin with oneself, a proper love of oneself. Gentleness leads to a good kind of order—order in the poustinia, order around it, a caring for the trees, the plants. The poustinik is possessed by a gentleness in loving himself, creation, and all others in the way God loves everything. God said that everything he made was very good, and the poustinik has a gentle care for this goodness.

You should always remember that the goal of the poustinia is to interiorize it. You must not think that the poustinia is the only place where you can be a poustinik. The Eastern tradition talks about "monasticism interiorized," which means that everyone is to live the life of the Trinity wherever they might be. Monasticism, in this sense, is for everyone.

My father was a layman. He lived as an ordinary man all his life. He enjoyed a good meal. But he also fasted a lot and prayed a great deal. He interiorized monasticism and fed his family with the scriptures and with the writings from the Fathers of the Desert. In like manner, the poustinia is a matter of the heart, and is for everyone.

Russia, as you know, is a very large country, and we like to roam around a great deal. And so we roam all over Russia with our pilgrimages. But one day you come to realize that all these geographical spaces are not enough, that they do not satisfy one's desire for space. At that point Russians begin the journey inward. This journey is far more beautiful and satisfies far more deeply. The poustinik, you might say, is involved in the great journey inward, exploring the vast spaces of God.

The poustinia is somehow always connected with the

notion of pilgrimage. The poustinik is an eternal pilgrim. Now a pilgrim cannot take along too much luggage. You can't take along 40 suitcases if you want to travel. Especially when we are talking of the journey of the poustinik — which is the journey inward, the journey toward the Trinity — we must travel lightly, taking only bread, salt, and water, symbols of our freedom of movement.

We have a saying that there are only three walls of a poustinia. The poustinik lives with one wall absent. At God's pleasure, in less than a second, he can be transported into any part of the world. His horizons are limitless. He begins to understand why he is in the poustinia. He begins to understand that he has been baptized to be the messenger of the Glad Tidings, and that his service is for the whole world and not only for his little village or apostolate.

Christ says to him: "Here is the way of the Cross. We are going to retrace all my footsteps, not in Palestine but in the whole world." One day the wall will fall down completely, and the poustinik will understand that his vocation is to "arise and go" while standing still! This is the mystery of the poustinia. He goes into the farthest reaches of the cosmos, standing still. That is his pilgrimage.

What is it to go into the cosmos? It's to be a messenger of God, following the one who sent him. The poustinik moves into the bloody footsteps of Christ and then he sees all around him the real tragedy of mankind. It is lack of faith in God. The daily cross of the poustinik will be to see this lack of faith, and especially among Christians. Every night he will return from his pilgrimage during which he stood so still, and on his back will be the cross of the day. Its special pain will be lack of faith, hope, and love. One day he will know that he must pray for faith, the next, hope, and then love. He will go forth from his poustinia day in and day out, or maybe it will be next month or next year. He waits on God's good pleasure. Sooner or later, however, the wall will fall down again, and his pilgrimage will begin—the strange pilgrimage of the poustinik that takes place while he is standing still.

The poustinik strives for the greatest poverty. There is a delightful little story about poverty from the Fathers. One of the monks named Serapion sold his book of the gospels and gave the money to those who were hungry. He said: "I have sold the book which told me to sell all that I had and give it to the poor."

I see Christ in poverty. He is most comfortable in poor places. He likes uncomfortable chairs; he likes to sleep on the floor. A good question to ask yourselves is whether he would be comfortable or not in your poustinias!

This doesn't mean that you shouldn't have comfort. That's not the most important point. It's more a matter of being totally detached from it. God is happy in simplicity and in poverty, especially poverty of spirit. A goal to strive for is when "the need to have becomes the need *not* to have."* It is an interiorization of poverty that desires with a passionate desire to get rid of everything. Sometimes this is not possible. But the desire is possible. We speak of the desire of baptism. There is also a "baptism of poverty," a passionate desire to be totally detached when total exterior poverty is not possible.

One of the hardest things to be detached from is our daily routine and life-style. Poustinikki, like everyone else, can become very attached to their horarium or daily schedule. Like everyone else, he has to have a horarium, times for getting up, cleaning, work, tending to his garden

_____

*The Struggle With God, p. 123.

—or whatever else he has to do. He has hours for prayer, and so on. But when you live alone it is so easy to attach yourself to your horarium, to what you are doing or have planned. It's easy to go around and say, "I'm busy for God," implying, "Don't bother me." No, the poustinik is one person who drops everything at the slightest knock at the door. This knock stands for all kinds of things. It may be a person knocking; it might also be God knocking. You must not forget that you went there for God and that God might knock at your door and enter just like anybody else. At that moment you must drop everything. You must be available especially for God.

How do you know if it is the Lord knocking? You don't. In the beginning there is lots of emotionalism, especially among women. It is difficult to sort out our own interruptions from those of the Lord. Let us say I am working at something. Suddenly, everything stops. I feel suddenly drawn to just stop. It's a very dangerous moment, exceedingly dangerous. The devil can draw you, and God can draw you. The Russian poustinik falls flat on his face and begins to pray. He is afraid of who might be drawing him, and where. But something happens within him that makes him feel that this is God. Now he just sits on the floor, on a chair, or wherever he is, and he is completely quiet. He listens in total silence. If it is Christ walking in, it is because he has something to say. Yes, when Christ comes in, he has something to say.

How does Christ speak? How did God speak to the prophets? Loud and clear, or was it more like a breeze that passed through their minds? It is possible for God to speak to us through our thoughts. The Russian poustinik will write them down and eventually ask his spiritual director about them. He has no faith in himself. This is one detachment that you have to have—total detachment from anything that might come to you through seemingly mystical phenomena. You have no faith in it until it is checked out by your spiritual director. Be very careful about such things, as you can enter into a tremendous amount of confusion and interior noise this way.

People often ask if they may study in the poustinia. What do they mean by the word "study"? Study God? Impossible. His chief study should be to ask the Lord, "Please teach me about yourself." He does this so that he may bring to the community the pure word of God.

But I know what question is being asked. They are asking about study "*academia*-style." Let me put it this way. I could see a poustinik studying after he has come to a point—and it's a strange point. It will need a bit of an explanation because it is part of the journey inward.

It's as if you were walking through a wide desert where there are only a few little water holes scattered here and there. You are staggering from thirst. You always have just enough water to survive. But now you begin to feel the weight of the desert, for the desert is God. You feel a terrible heaviness and you feel more thirsty. You want the consolation of God, an emotional gimmick of some sort, you want help. You haven't reached the stage yet where you want God himself. God will give us little holes of water along the way, but he loves us too much to give us any other artificial supports.

The water is faith. As you move from hole to hole the water becomes fresher and you have the feeling that you can really move now. Now faith begins to grow in you. You begin to understand that faith is not of the understanding, but is a gift of God. Your throat becomes unparched. The water in each hole now is neither bitter nor salty, but fresh. Now you can stand up, whereas before you were practically crawling from hole to hole. You can walk straight toward the next hole because faith has increased in you by the grace of the Holy Spirit, through the gift of the Father. Now you walk like a man or a woman walks—straight.

The last hole is the biggest yet. You have enough to assuage your thirst, and you know that somewhere, someplace, you are going to be covered and inundated by faith. It will burst in on you like a sudden revelation and you will realize that you are a baptized, that is, a saved Christian.

That's when you suddenly arrive at a beautiful river. You come to the edge of it and know that you can drink from it until you die. Now faith has taken hold of you and nothing, nothing, nothing can separate you from the river. You realize that through your journey you have fallen in love with God, and that it was really his face you saw in each water hole. The water holes were God's gift of faith to you, for God alone could quench your thirst. *When the poustinik has arrived at this river of faith, then he can study.* Then he will never be misled by what he studies.

To continue with this image of the desert: The poustinia means desert—is a desert. Why does anyone want to go to a desert? To follow Christ. The desert is the land of detachment. To follow Christ is to deny ourselves. The first kind of detachment in the poustinia is from oneself. I think that the greatest challenge of the poustinia is this detachment from oneself. This is not simply detachment from my "will," as some Western spiritual writers put it, it's detachment from many things. From food, from studies. But even more than all these material things, it's the ability to take out a boat that has no rudder and no oars. It's the ability to drift wherever God wants to lead you. One of the characteristics of a poustinik is this ability to let yourself go wherever God wants to lead you. I may come to a nice little river where I would like to stop and have lunch! Wssssh, a storm comes up! So I don't stop to eat but head into the storm. It's this going with God wherever he wants to take you that is the essence of detachment.

The question arises sometimes whether a poustinik can write. You live in the poustinia for three days, of course you can write, why shouldn't you write? All the things I've been reading to you were written by the great poustinikki, from the czars down to the paupers.

If someone asks if he can come to see you, don't ask why. Simply say, "I'd be delighted to be of any help to you that I can." (Stress the word "help"!)

If such a person comes in and sits down, it may become apparent very soon that he has only come out of curiosity. You are not in the poustinia to satisfy curiosity seekers. If they are simply asking questions like "Where do you come from? How long have you been here?"—cut them off gently but firmly. Try to get them to pray with you. This is what I call the "courtesy of the poustinia." It is your duty to make the other person aware that the place you are in is holy. Your approach in such a situation will be a mixture of courtesy, gentleness, tenderness—while using a scalpel! People should not come to you simply for a cup of tea and a little gossip.

Perhaps this would be a good place to discuss the poustinia as a dwelling. First and foremost, a poustinik is not a solitary. In the English language, the word solitary means "alone." In the Russian language *it means to be with everybody*. A solitary person, for a Russian, is a hospice, an inn, for every person. It is not simply a question of "loving humanity." In some sense, one wall of the poustinia is entirely open, and the poustinik is *in* Bangladesh, or India, or Northern Ireland. Every Father of the Eastern Church has practiced this kind of hospitality.

Hospitality has to be total. It is not enough to share your bread or your tea or your coffee with whoever comes to visit, though this is the first kind of hospitality offered. Thus when a person comes in, the first thing you offer is food. We live by food. Without food we cannot exist. God comes to us as food. Almost in the same act of opening the door, the poustinik asks, "Have you eaten? Can I share something with you?" In Russia we would say, "May I offer you what God in his mercy has sent me?"

I remember once pilgrimaging with my mother. We came to a household. All the family had were a large loaf of black bread and some yogurt. There was hardly enough food for the family, but when we came in they cut it so we could have a share. Even if there's nothing to give, we can still offer a cup of water.

So hospitality is first and foremost of this practical kind. The ideal to strive for, however, is hospitality of the heart. It is the serene acceptance of any and all interruptions by visitors whom you may not even know personally. Some visitors you should especially accept because they can teach you something. It is very important to have a serenity about hospitality, a sort of peace that radiates much like the offering of food creates a feeling of fellowship. Actual food is, however, only the first step. Christ said that man cannot live by bread alone. The poustinik should practice this by also offering himself.

What does a Russian mean by offering himself? It means a kenosis, an emptying of myself in order to be filled with the other. We in the East consider every person to be

Christ, in an exaggerated sort of way. This point is well exemplified in a little story found in the book, *What Men Live By*.

It concerns a man who was told, through prayer, that Christ was going to visit him on a certain day. He went about his business as usual; he was a shoemaker. His first customer was a prostitute, the second a mother with a sick child, the third was an alcoholic. He hurried around, trying to be hospitable to all these people. When evening came he was rather disappointed. It was time to lock up—and Christ still hadn't come. He was very unhappy. Suddenly he heard a voice, "But I had come, in the person of each of the people to whom you offered hospitality today." Thus must the poustinik see Christ in each person who comes to him.

Thus the poustinik must be completely available to everyone. He is available to God during the days he is in the poustinia, as well as being available to the community. It is so easy for the poustinik to say, "I am entitled to three days in my poustinia where I can have a life of my own. Then I'll give four days of service to the community." No, he may be called upon at any time to help his brother. He is completely indifferent to his prayer being interrupted, to being called hither and yon. He is indifferent because he is absorbed in the prayer of the presence of God (which is the Jesus Prayer for the Russian). So, as far as he is concerned, he is walking out of the poustinia and remaining in it—if you know what I mean. He is eternally in a poustinia. That is the very essence of the poustinia. Men went into the poustinia to learn the prayer of the presence of God. When you have this presence of God in your heart, you have a poustinia in your heart, and then you are a light to the world.

In order to be available, the poustinik must be *flexible*. Flexibility flows from the fact that he is beginning to live in eternity and in the *freedom of Christ*. He is unperturbed about himself and about what is happening to him. He adapts easily. He never stands on ceremony. All this flows from his freedom. He realizes that a totality of dependence on God and totality of surrender to him is true freedom. It is an entirely different freedom from the kind that men usually speak about. It is a freedom of total subjection to God. It is a freedom of the silent heart which is constantly moved by the thought of God and his desires. It is the freedom of a person who sees in every face God's face. It's the freedom of a person who cannot be angered because his idea of himself is such that he considers any insult a compliment.

A poustinik is known by his fruits. One of the fruits of the poustinia is a defenselessness which flows from his freedom. If someone walks over you with hobnailed boots on, you kiss his feet and say, "Thank you very much for treating me like this, for I am a sinner." The poustinik is like a rubber ball. The worse you treat him the harder he bounces back! You just can't keep him down. One of the poustinik's great contributions to the community is a real example of defenselessness, of forgiveness.

A poustinik is a living forgiveness. You cannot hurt him. He is tempered like steel, refined like silver seven times. In the poustinia something happens. The poustinik becomes supple through hardness and hard through being supple.

The poustinia is a place for resting in the Lord. The Lord says to us, "Go into the inward journey of your heart, and I shall be your rest." You are not cognizant of any kind of mystical resting on the bosom of God. It's just plain, plumb rest. We Russians used to talk about this in New York. We had a very rough time when we first came. We were overworked and underpaid. We used to discuss among ourselves how we survived. We came to the conclusion that we survived because we really believed that God was our rest. When I asked a friend of mine, "How do we survive?" this is exactly what she said: "Oh, we have Christ for a pillow." The poustinik comes to experience this kind of resting in the arms of the Lord.

The final result of all these attitudes is peace. The sign by which you know a good poustinik is peace. Whether he knows it or not, he exudes an intense peace. He is so peaceful that just being next to him has a settling effect. There are very few people in the world with whom you feel at peace. There are very few people who encompass you with peace as with a mantle. The poustinik is supposed to be not only a peace-maker, but a peace-giver.

9

Confrontation with Evil and Martyrdom

The desert, as understood in Eastern spirituality, is also the dwelling place of Satan. We know from the gospels that he dwells there, and that that is where he tempted the Lord himself. The three great temptations of Christ happened in the desert. The desert thus has deep significance in Christian spirituality. The Jews were led 40 years through the desert. Abraham was called to the desert, to a pilgrimage of faith. I need not repeat all the instances in the New Testament in which the desert is mentioned.

When I speak about desert in connection with the poustinik, I am not talking about the literal desert of heat and sand. I speak about someone—the poustinik—who goes into a hidden place to be alone with the great silence of God, to learn to know God as God reveals himself. God reveals himself to the poustinik in response to the latter's love. The poustinik waits in poverty, surrender, and in the knowledge that he is one of the anawim, a real poor man in the spirit of the beatitudes. This desert dweller knows that he is there not only for himself but for the rest of humanity. He understands that he must take humanity with him in his prayers and tears and that his cabin is also the dwelling place of humanity. He understands his prophetic vocation: He listens only in order to pass on that which is given to him. He understands that he has no lock on his door, only a latch against the wind, but never against any human being. He understands that he must *share* that which is given to him by Christ with other people. All this is clear to him.

The poustinik also foresees that he is going to meet Satan. In the beginning he doesn't know how often these meetings are going to take place. This is hidden from him. But he knows that inevitably, sooner or later, the Evil One will come to tempt him.

In the Eastern tradition, temptations are stepping-stones. It seems ridiculous to compare them to school "grades," but God allows men to be tempted so that they may grow in faith, love, and hope. It's as if God puts us through a school of love. Our passing from grade to grade is our reaction to and our overcoming of the temptations which he permits the devil to try us with. The Lord wants us to grow in faith and love of him, trusting in him alone. He wants us to absorb, with our whole being, his words, "Fear not—I have overcome the world," "In me, the Prince of this world has nothing," and "Fear not, little flock, I shall be with you to the end of time." He wants us to experience, with St. Paul, that "My grace is sufficient for you." All this is what he wants to teach us, and therefore he allows Satan, who roams in a dark and waterless desert of his own, to come out to the desert and the poustinik.

For those who go into the desert for any length of time, or who have the vocation to dwell there for many years, these temptations will come. The temptations might be subtle, like the whispering of leaves on the trees, like the rushing of shifting sands on the dunes, like the rustling noises in a forest. They may come in cries, like the baying of a coyote in the distance. They may come without sounds, but they will come. And suddenly, the poustinia will become fearsome. The house will seem to close in on the poustinik. Quite unexpectedly, the Holy Book will become just a jumble of letters, mere words and sentences which no amount of praying will be able to connect with anything else in the mind and heart of the desert dweller.

In the night, fear will come to dwell with him who dwells in the poustinia. The place will become cold on the hottest days. There will be a desire to run away from the poustinia, to get among people, to get away from the loneliness that has suddenly taken possession of the heart which only a moment ago seemed to be united with God. Suddenly, it is as if God had never been there. There is nothing but a shack, a log cabin. Its poverty seems more distasteful and grim than ever.

The night will be barely endurable. Prayer will become impossible. Sleep has fled, seemingly never to return. An almost physical, palpable fear reaches to a fever pitch and takes hold of one. The uselessness of such a life suddenly becomes quite evident, and the person begins to wonder why he is in this desert place. "Why has God led us into this desert place?" (Ex 16:3). What folly brought them here? Again and again the mind is centered on getting out, getting out from under everything that now appears completely senseless.

Yes, Satan might come under these guises. Or, he might enter the intellect and, with clear and irrefutable logic, prove that the poustinik is wasting his life, that he or she would do so much more good among his fellowmen, and that he should leave this utterly foolish vocation. Sometimes the power is given to Satan to try and persuade the poustinik that it isn't a vocation at all, that it is all an illusion. This agony of the mind is even worse than terror and panic. It is as if an edifice were crumbling, as if the person himself were crumbling. Yes, Satan can come in this guise too.

Or, he can come in the guise of pride. The poustinik might really think that he is a wise man, wise with his own wisdom, and that he should go and preach to others now—now that he is "ready."

The Evil One can use sex, mind, body, soul, anything, to twist and turn, to disturb the peace of the poustinik. He can literally come *into* the house where his presence will be felt, sensed, and the means of getting rid of him will suddenly be lost. It is impossible to describe all the vile ways of Satan. He is able to quote scripture or turn into an angel of light.

Also, under the guise of inspiration, the devil may entice you to all kinds of extraordinary works. Throw them out. God does not demand extraordinary works unless your spiritual director asks for them. Consult your spiritual director about anything that appears above the level of ordinary spiritual life.

Periods of temptation may be long or short. This depends on God's permissive will. But they will be there. There will be moments of darkness, of lostness, of loneliness, of agony, of fear, of questioning, of doubts, of terror, and of panic. Against these things there is only one answer: to stand still and say the Jesus Prayer, even though each letter of that simple prayer weighs a ton! Make the sign of the cross, and kiss the icon of Mary, the Mother of God.

Stand still . . . don't run away! Stand Still! Such is what writers in Eastern spirituality offer as a remedy against the temptations of the devil. They also recommend more fasting, some bodily penance perhaps, but above all they counsel this standing still. It is in such standing still that faith grows, hope comes alive, and love deepens. If anyone thinks that he can enter the poustinia and live there without meeting Satan, then let him not enter the poustinia. If he does enter the poustinia, let him not count on his own strength of mind and soul. Rather, let him admit more keenly and more simply that he is a sinner, a poor man, one of the anawim, and because of this he must lean more on God, like a drowning man reaches out to a floating log.

In this knowledge—that without God we can do nothing—we reach a high point of understanding. This becomes the moment of real believing when we experience in the darkness, in the fear, in the terror, in the panic, that his grace is indeed sufficient for us. We come to see that if God has permitted the tempter to come to us, then God will give us the grace to resist him.

Yes, these are the great moments of growth in faith, hope, and charity that God sends to the poustinik. These are also the moments when the poustinik is really fighting for the world, for he is attacked, as it were, in the name of humanity. As at these times he knows himself to be extremely human, so at the same time he knows that God gives him special graces to fight these temptations, not only for himself but for all humanity. Always the poustinik knows that he is in the poustinia for others, and that his prayers, his mortifications, his being exposed to temptations, his meetings with Satan—all these are experienced by him as a representative of humanity. For the poustinik lives in Christ, and Christ took humanity upon himself. So too, by the grace of God, the poustinik takes all of humanity upon himself, and becomes, with the help of God, a holocaust for all men. He becomes a Simon of Cyrene, a Veronica. A poustinik is never alone. The whole world is with him and it is for that world that he weeps, mortifies himself, enters the silence of God, fights the temptations of Satan. All these things are never for himself alone!

This aspect of the spirituality of the poustinik is terribly important. It's the very reason why in Russia we say that this vocation is *given* to someone. A community rejoices that God has chosen someone out of their midst because their faith tells them that his vocation is precisely *for them*. The poustinik's whole reason for going into loneliness, into solitude—his whole reason for exposing himself to temptations, is always for others. It is always an identification with the holocaust of Christ, with his whole life, with his crucifixion. It is the way to *our* resurrection and that of others. For we die in Christ and we resurrect in Christ, not only through baptism, but through the fruit of baptism—faith, hope, and love. The men and women whom God has called to be alone with him in his immense silence and to be his prophets must understand that well, with his help and that of Our Lady!

The road is long and hard and difficult. Never be afraid. You won't be if you understand where you are and why you are there. You won't be afraid—but you might be awed. Somewhere along the road you will meet evil. For whenever God reveals himself, he must allow you to meet the other one, who is also part of his creation. It is not that you are grasping at the forbidden fruit of the tree, but God allows a confrontation with it. You have to know how to encounter evil at God's bidding, at his time, in order to be able to contribute to the community of man. For evil is among us. You will understand how to handle evil or the Evil One because God has put upon you the

robe and the ring, and you have come close to the Trinity—
you have been drawn into him.

So now you will be tempted, but you won't be afraid.
If you are afraid, then you had better have a talk with your
spiritual director. Then the dimension that we are discussing has not yet happened in you. There is a connection between God's teaching you about himself and the
encounter he permits you to have with evil.

How do you overcome evil? Again, by faith. It is by
the sign of the cross, the invocation of Our Lady's name.
the name of Jesus, but above all by faith. For when you
encounter evil you know God exists. I don't know if I am
making myself clear on this point. Physically and emotionally you might be afraid. You may perspire. You must
disregard these things. The next step is the invitation to
faith. God is calling you to come up higher, and Christ,
'your brother, is saying to you: "Yes, this is the Evil One,
but I am here, and I have conquered evil and death on
the Cross. So give me your hand and the Evil One will be
but a stepping-stone to where you wish to go." So in faith,
you put your hand into Christ's hand and you walk over,
symbolically speaking, the back of the devil. He's just a
stepping-stone. But you have to believe that Christ has extended his hand, because then you will be utterly unafraid.

Such things will happen to you again and again, but
they are not to be feared if you believe. As a poustinik
you figuratively and sometimes factually prostrate yourself
and cry out, "Lord, I believe, help my unbelief." He will
help you. The poustinia is God's constant school of love.
When you have finished with this school, explosions like the
atom bomb will be like toys to you. You probably will not
realize exactly who you are, what has happened to you.
But people will come to the place where you are. You

will be going out to make your contribution because now you know that *you* don't, *he* does.

Thus the poustinik is always moving slowly into a deeper understanding of *martyrdom*. Martyrdom has many faces.

Perhaps sometime in the tomorrows of Madonna House, evil, really evil people will come. God will let you know that they are evil. You will not be afraid because somehow you will see Christ even in them. Who knows, you may even be killed. If so, with your last breath you must say, "My Lord and my God, Alleluia!" Charles de Foucauld understood this kind of senseless martyrdom. He was uselessly killed by a group of Tuaregs in the Sahara to whom he had done no harm. He was truly a poustinik with an open door; he accepted this martyrdom and did not run away. He didn't even try to protect himself. He lived out his interior martyrdom.

There is another kind of martyrdom. Most of us will not be martyred in the way that Charles de Foucauld experienced. But a poustinik will be a martyr of another sort, and he must be prepared for it. It is the martyrdom of facing oneself, one's emotional self. No one wants to face his emotional self. Nobody wants to admit that he or she acts at times like a 10-year-old, that they have a thousand different moods, that they are afraid of the silliest things. We don't like to face these facts. This is the beginning of our martyrdom.

Then Christ comes in. Remember that the poustinia door has no latch. That means that Christ too can come in! He enters and says, "Come, let us go a little farther on our journey." The second stage of the journey toward martyrdom is being torn apart between your emotional states and knowing yourself as you are. It's a very deep martyrdom.

The third stage is an ability to really face oneself without all the emotional camouflage. Though painful, it is a stage so filled with grace that, in a sense, it ceases to be a martyrdom and becomes a sort of oneness with God. Now, one looks at one's sins truly and honestly. That looking is another phase of the martyrdom. But one is no longer in any despair or is upset. The martyrdom is being oiled by the love of God. It no longer rubs abrasively, hurtfully. There descends an understanding that all martyrdom in this area of self-knowledge is one of the greatest graces that God can give us. The poustinia gives birth to that grace. Outside the poustinia it is more difficult to acquire it because too many things distract us— and because we desire to be distracted.

Some people may think that such self-knowledge will lead to depression. For a Russian, depression in a poustinia is impossible. A person who tends toward such a depressive complex will not choose the poustinia. He will choose a pilgrimage, because he is restless, unhappy; he has to keep moving all the time. Furthermore, a community is very aware of depressed people. They wouldn't want to have them around. In Russia they would write to a bishop or someone to say that something is wrong with the poustinik!

The martyrdom continues. We are beginning to know who we are. We are beginning to be at home in our difficulties, with our sins, seeing more clearly what they are. A strange clarity comes, a clarity of soul. I imagine that for Westerners it will take quite a bit of time to reach this clarity of soul.

Clarity of soul is different from clarity of mind. I can see my sins clearly with my mind. I can use the methods recommended by ascetical theology (which is based on reason) to overcome my sins. But clarity of soul is acquired by the *gift of tears*. I weep, and the tears wash away my sins and the sins of others. My mind is serene and unaffected, because I know that the grace of tears is not from my mind but proceeds from the heart of God. It comes to my heart, and I weep. My mind now is clear and my heart is clear—I am clear. You must never forget (and the poustinia gives you this understanding), that when *I* weep, *Christ* weeps, because Christ is in me. When my tears mingle with those of Christ, then *his holiness* washes me, not mine.

Again, we should distinguish between depression and a state of sorrow. Sorrow is a state of union with God in the pain of men. It is a state of deep and profound understanding. It is as if God put his hand out and the panorama of the whole world and its pain is opened before you. This is the action of the Holy Spirit. The gift of tears flows— not the gift of tongues, but the gift of tears. The tears are such that you cannot stop them—nor should you try. You must allow them to flow. They will stop—just like that— when God wants them to stop. These are tears of sorrow, but they are not for yourself. They are not tears of anger, or tears of animosity toward anyone. These are very pure tears, not subject to your control. You can neither begin them nor stop them. But neither are you upset by them.

When tears come to my eyes in this way I do not investigate where they're from, whom they're for, and so on. I believe in faith that they are from God, that I am crying with him because he cares for me and cries with me. Sometimes when I go to church I am in a perfectly happy mood. I do a little skip, pick up a flower or two. I'm fine. I arrive at the church. I kneel down. I'm happy to be at Mass. Suddenly, without any action on my part, I begin to cry

Why do I cry? Nothing told me I should cry. No unfortunate or sorrowful incident happened between my waking and coming to church. It's as spontaneous as the wind. I just cry—and it's uncontrollable. I have no way of stopping it. I just continue to cry. I've tried to stop it. Nothing works. Slowly it stops.

Afterwards I don't know why I cried or what started or stopped it. But I know that it came from God. Something happened in the world that made God cry and he invited me to cry. Or perhaps I cried and invited him to cry. It has something to do with the exceeding holiness of God, not me. All the tears wash away my sins and the sins of the world. When this happens, you have nothing to do with it. If it happens of your own will or because of your own emotions, it's not tears from God. They are somebody else's tears, but not God's. They're your own tears. Poustinikki are more prone to shedding the tears of God because their lives are so concentrated on God. It always happens unexpectedly, without knowing when or how or why. It's suddenly there.

This brings us back to clarity of soul again. The clarity achieved by these tears does not mean that now the soul is sinless, nor, of course, does it mean we are saints. It just means that my soul has been cleansed by God, that I have been able to recognize who I am—with all my arrogance, my pride, my self-will. It doesn't mean that tomorrow we will not be arrogant, proud, etc. But we have reached some new level where we can recognize that the arrogance is there, and the recognition leads us closer to God. This is clarity of soul.

Russians believe that the greatest purity is achieved through tears, tears that really wash us. Our tears mingle with the tears of Christ and cleanse the soul of every extraneous thing that is bothering it. Tears wash away every interior attachment which hinders true poverty of spirit.

Tears are also another way through which we come to appreciate the great gift of God: our freedom. Our soul, washed by tears, can see clearly that we really are free, that we can say yes or no to God. In the poustinia, this struggle between yes and no, this struggle with God, is intensified a hundredfold. At some point, your yes to God will make you nonexistent. It's only a second. Something will happen in your purified soul through these tears and struggles. You will seem to be like one dead. But it won't last long. You will return, and on that day you will know a miracle. You made your choice for God. The true liberation that God reserves for those who love him will be yours.

The Lord, from time immemorial, has known you. He has allowed his fire to come down upon you like a crimson dove. His fire is over you. You are moving slowly up to his mountain, the mountain of the Lord. To get there you must pass through the heart of God. As you pass through his heart, you become a bonfire, and, together, a huge bonfire. You become a bonfire on the top of the mountain. Many people see it and come to find out what it is. So they climb the mountain too; they come to your poustinias. They see that you are very strange bonfires. Transparent. You are a bonfire through which they can go. At the other end the heart of Christ is waiting for them. Having been yourselves scooped up by the hand of God, and having agreed to it by your yes, you have now become a transparent bonfire that leads other men to Christ.

10

Liberation in Christ

"God said, 'Let us make man in our own image, in the likeness of ourselves, and let him be master of the fish, of the sea, the birds of the air, the cattle, all the wild beasts, and all the reptiles that crawl upon the earth.' God created man in the image of himself, in the image of God he created him, male and female he created them."

While I was in the poustinia of the Little Sisters of Charles de Foucauld in Montreal the words that came to me out of the poustinia were simple and yet complex— freedom and liberation. Since then I have thought a lot about them, because I didn't have time to set them down as I usually do here at Madonna House. The poustinia at the Little Sisters is a bit different from here. So I kept the words in my heart and let them cling to me, trying to discover what they meant. It came to me that God had created all the earth and then he wanted to create man. "Let us make man in our own image and likeness." What is the image and likeness of God but love and freedom? By creating man he endowed him with a free will because God is free and he created man in his own image.

I'm not a theologian. I'm just a person who tries to listen to the words of God and meditate on them. It struck me that God wanted someone like himself to "talk things over with," as the scriptures say. Why did God give us freedom? Because he wanted to be freely loved. He loved us deeply because he created us. The act of creation is an act of love. But we know that God extended his act of love further than creation. He sent his Son to become a holocaust for us. The suffering servant of Yahweh was a bridge, a restorer, for at some point we misused our freedom. So the love of God extended into great depths and so did his gift to us, the gift of free will and freedom. I, as a Christian, must choose and should choose and will choose that which God wants me to choose freely, namely his will.

It struck me, as I meditated on this freedom God gave us, that it was unlimited in the sense that we had the power to say "no" to God as well as "yes." For a long time I pondered over these words, no and yes. The more I pondered, the more I was awed that I did have this fantastic freedom of saying yes and no to God. Because I had this power I was God's heir, I was the sister of Christ, since I had been baptized into his death and resurrected life. Somehow, even before I was his child, I had it, because I was created in his image and likeness.

I looked at my hands, though my hands had nothing really to do with this whole thing. But I looked at my hands because hands are used to hold, and somehow my hands held freedom. I looked long and hard and meditated in the depths of the night on what my hands held. I knew also what sin was. Sin was really the turning of my back on God, the definite "no" to his love, the surrender to someone else who was not God. Sin was a chaining of my freedom even though I was free to say this no. When I said no something happened *to me* and *because of* me. But I was still free to say no.

On the other hand, if I said yes, as I was free to do, something else happened. I walked into a sort of sunrise. My pilgrimage toward the Absolute became suffused with light instead of darkness (as it did with the "no"). This freedom of mine when I said yes became a song that I sang with God. There is a song today which goes, "I am the Lord of the dance." I felt like singing, "I am the Lord of the song." When I say yes and use my freedom to really be free, I become one with the whole song of creation.

The more I meditated on freedom the more things I discovered. First I discovered that I *was* free. This was the foundation of my meditation. No one was pushing me, no one was telling me what to do. I presume that I am a Christian who understands her religion and who has taken part in the sacraments and has lived the life of the Church. (For I am speaking now of Christians.) So as a Christian I meditated on this gift of freedom. God is here, and I can love him or not. I can be hot, cold, or tepid toward him.

I am free to choose, to act, and for this freedom I rejoice and thank God, even though I know the terrific responsibility of it, the total insecurity of it also. For *I* have to decide—that is so very important. True, I can have advisors, spiritual directors, books, but ultimately, in the great reality of my relation to God and men, I alone must make the decision when the time comes. That is freedom.

So God gives us freedom. I meditate a little deeper. In fact, the meditation ceases and a sort of quiet enters my soul, heart, and mind. In that quiet, that silence, that beautiful silence of God who allows me to enter into it and become silent myself, my horizon expands and I see a fantastically immense horizon of unsurpassed beauty. It lies alongside a desert. On one side is the desert of the power of Satan whose one desire is to bind my will to do his will. On the other side there is the Lord, the Trinity. The Holy Spirit, the Crimson Dove, the God of love, hovers over me like an immense and flaming bird. Perhaps it's not a bird at all. Perhaps it's a fire that I mistake for a bird. Quietly, in total and utter stillness, Christ stands there beside me somewhere, but leading to the Father as he usually does.

The more I behold this freedom of mine, poised between these two choices, the more tired I get. Everything suddenly becomes very clear, very simple, and that kind of simplicity is intensely tiring to us human beings. For the vision is clear. There is the burning desert, and there is the other side of the desert which appears so restful. I am somewhere in between. I must decide to go either to the right, into the will of the Father, or to the left, into my own will and into the desert of Satan. Yes, I am tired because the sight is so clear. I see confusion and demonic powers calling me to do my will contrary to the will of God.

Then, suddenly, all these thoughts leave my mind and I simply realize that God has given me the freedom of choice and a free will, and that he has sent his Son to show me how to do his will. That is what his Son came down to do—to do the will of the Father freely, without compulsion, at the request, as it were, of his Father. I was like that too, like Jesus. I had a free will, and I was not being compelled.

Now my mind begins to clear and my meditation becomes simple. Yes, I am the sister of Jesus Christ. Yes, I have come to do the will of the Father. Yes, that is what I am going to do. I have made the decision. I know that my *fiat* will have to be repeated again and again, but I am ready, with the grace of God, to do so.

At this moment a strange, indescribable sensation comes over me. Because in accepting the will of the Father I surrender all things to him—father, mother, brothers, sisters, relatives, the life that I lead—in short, everything. Once I have decided to put my will into the immense sea of Christ's will, I seem to come to a moment of non-existence, and there are no ways in which I can put it into words. It is as if by total surrender of my will I also surrender my body, my mind, my senses, everything that is me, and I am as if I were not.

Suddenly I come out of this nonexistence and I look at myself. I realize that I have been changed in the twinkling of an eye. Now indeed I am free. I am not worried about anything anymore. I am like a bird soaring in the air and all things are mine because all things are God's and I am his too. Now I am unbound. I repeat, I am unbound. I am free like the air. I possess everything and God possesses me. Now my free will blends with his and a strange fire enters my soul. Now I understand that a will freely given to God becomes transformed by a joyous and fantastic zeal in the service of God and his Church. Now indeed I step easily and simply into the steps of him who calls himself "the Lord of the dance," and I sing to him and with him whose music is given to the world only as an echo, for all music is an echo of God's music. Now I suddenly understand that by using my free will freely I entered God. The reason for using free will is love, and the gift of love was given to me in the gift of faith. Now in love and in faith I sing of hope.

It is all so very simple, my dear ones. I bring you the words that I heard without hearing, the sights that I saw without seeing; I bring you the results of man's right choice: the gift of liberation. Now I am free. I am lib-

erated. Alleluia! Alleluia! Alleluia! For I have surrendered, and while I surrendered, all my bonds have
been cut. Behold, I am free. In union with the will of
God I soar, I dance, I sing. But above all, day in and
day out, I do his will. Alleluia! Alleluia!

The poustinia, then, is the place of freedom, the freedom which *I* am very conscious of exercising. It's *I* who
decided to go into the poustinia. It's a way of freely declar-
ing that I love God and a way of showing it. I say to him:
"Now look. Very freely, without any coercion, I'm going
a little further than other people. I don't know what it's
all about yet, but I know it's a place that will bring me
closer to you. Because I am falling in love with you, I want
to come closer to you of my own free will." If you stay in
the poustinia, there will be a *liberation*.

What's the difference between freedom and liberation?
Liberation comes from Christ. It's the freedom that God
gives you because you have freely accepted him—it's a
gift of God. It's a fantastic thing. It has made you free.
When *I* choose to go to the poustinia, to fast, to pray, to
be faithful to the Roman Catholic Church and to God—
when *I* choose to do those things—that's freedom. But
liberation comes from God.

He says to us, "Now that you have really tried, I'll give
myself to you to a degree and in a way that you have never
suspected possible." He liberates you from the things that
"bugged" you. It's very funny. Not that the things that
bugged you cease to bug you. They still are there to bug
you, but you don't care about them anymore. You have
been liberated by this gift of God. You have reached the
apex of that freedom which you can give God, then suddenly, he gives you his liberation. People may still annoy
me, but somehow they do not affect me. I have been

liberated by God. It's as if I were traveling through the cosmos of the Lord all by myself. It's as if everything that now comes across my path has a reason in God's plan for being there. It's as if the gift of discernment has become a sixth sense. Life used to be heavy and difficult. Now it is light and natural.

The gift of wisdom is also part of this liberation. Discernment and wisdom—the gifts which relate especially to people—coalesce and make me free from all the things that try to pull me down. At no time does the poustinik think that he has achieved this by himself, or that there is any way of achieving it by himself except by the constant, free, following of Christ.

When a poustinik enters a poustinia he really faces himself. Much of the gospel is concerned with this facing of oneself. Christ said that it is what comes out of a man that defiles him. We are not able to face what is inside us. The poustinik is the free man. He enters there of his own free will, to face himself. Many things, but especially the devil, will conspire to force you to leave the poustinia—to block this confrontation with yourself.

Perhaps I can put it this way: When you enter the poustinia you enter the orbit of God. You hold on to his coat. A thousand hands try to pull his coat out of your hands. You are free to give in to the temptation, to flee from the poustinia, or to resist.

It's because of this freedom that a poustinik has no rules. There is nothing to guide yourself by except what is within. This is where discernment comes in. Among the variety of things that people want you to do, you have to discern from your heart what to do. Your life ought to be a life of service to the communiy. There is only one thing you do *not* do: satisfy your own ego.

The essence of the poustinia is freedom, total freedom of action, directed by your love of God and God's love for you. Should you do this, should you do that? Consult your heart! Put your head into your heart, get down on your knees, prostrate yourself or whatever you do, and find the answer from God. Most of the duties will be obvious. But precisely because you have this freedom, the poustinik should be the most obedient of all. When something is really necessary (in the apostolate), he should be the one who runs to the task with the greatest joy.

The poustinik has no security because he depends entirely on God. God tends to turn our lives upside down every three minutes. The poustinik must have the freedom to break any routine he might have at a moment's notice.

The same freedom is present in relation to Christ. Christ is present in the poustinia. You came to encounter him there. He draws us with his ointments and with his beautiful aromas. Sometimes this attraction in the poustinia is so powerful that you can almost touch it. But along with this positive attraction, there is always an opposite attraction. So I have to exercise my free will again, my freedom, to move toward Christ or away from him every second of the day in the poustinia. The poustinia is present to give eternally new dimensions to these attractions of Christ.

Darkness also comes into the poustinia. Up until now I may have walked in the light, or in the twilight. It wasn't so bad. I could distinguish things for myself. (Remember that I am always talking about the eyes and ears of the heart.) Suddenly I'm confronted with what St. John of the Cross calls darkness. I must make a decision whether or not I am going to freely enter that darkness. Here is where the poustinik usually stops facing the darkness. I stand there and must take my first step freely into that night.

This is the time of the spiritual director, because it's a time when we are tempted to run away. This is the time for all sorts of rationalization. This is the time when I am tempted to process everything through my head instead of through my heart. Many forces will marshal themselves to prevent you from entering that darkness. The role of the spiritual director is important here because the territory ahead is unknown and uncharted.

Then, by the grace of God (the gift of liberation), and by your own free will (freedom), without being forced in any way, you enter into the darkness. What do I mean "by your own free will"? I mean that there is no inner fear. There is no fear that God is displeased with you. Freedom here joins with faith and knows that God is never displeased with you. Jesus has changed all that.

Or, the temptation may work in the opposite way. "I am here in the poustinia and I am supposed to be here. If I don't enter into this night, then I will displease God." Confusion is always from the devil. This last thought doesn't seem to limit your freedom, but it does nonetheless. The Evil One is already lassoing you. You've got to be very careful here. Never move on *any* idea of guilt or any kind of rationality at all. Freedom means freedom.

So you enter that dark night. You brace yourself. This is the moment when you really and literally fold the wings of your intellect, but totally. Now you have to go through a painful process painful even for an Eastern person who may be more used to it than you. There is an emptying of the mind as you enter this dark night. One must walk without any mind. In a sense, we could say that only fools (which in some English translations means mad people in-sane without minds") walk into and open themselves deliberately to this night.

There is a strange emptiness toward which one moves. It doesn't happen in a day. I realize that part of the effort is mine. I seem to latch onto a little bit of something. I don't know what it is. It helps me to fold the wings of my intellect and empty a little bit more of myself. St. John of the Cross says, "I jumped into the abyss and caught my prey." The poustinik jumps into the abyss and may not necessarily catch his prey. But he still must jump into that emptiness. Frankly, it's one of the most painful things. It's not painful to quiet your thoughts and all those other preliminary things. That's relatively easy. It's when this emptiness takes hold of you, or you allow it to take hold of you (I don't know which); then for a moment or two you seem to cease to exist.

Sartre talks much about moving toward nothingness. But Sartre really *has* nothing. There is nothing behind his nothingness. It's just despair. It's the end. Christianity moves into this "nothingness" and finds God. There comes a moment in this movement toward nothingness which seems to be a moment of nonexistence. It appears idiotic, positively idiotic to say such a thing. But it's true. It's a moment in which you are nonexistent as far as being a person is concerned. Everything has disappeared. You are not even cognizant that "you are." You are only cognizant of darkness. Whether you are in depths or heights is unimportant; you are not even cognizant of that. But there is a moment of nonexistence out of which you come. And when you come out, prayer begins.

This moment of nonexistence is short, exceedingly short. It hits you and is gone. But after that, prayer begins. Now it's a very strange prayer. It's a prayer that is no prayer, because it takes place in an *interiorized passivity*. It has no connection with what you are doing—walking, sleeping, whatever. In you now there is a tremendous change. Prayer now begins to make sense because you don't pray; God prays in you. This is where true liberation enters. Up till now, freedom has been operating. You've submitted yourself to God of your own free will. Now he takes over, and that's where true liberation begins.

All these struggles bring us back again, as it were, to the Trinity, to whom we must bring ourselves by the scruff of our necks. We know there is a great reluctance to go to the Trinity. Why? Because we know that our surrender is not total. There are moments in our lives, especially in the poustinia, when God reminds us of the hidden corners in our souls and minds that we haven't surrendered to him. This, I think, is what I mean by picking yourself up by the scruff of your neck and bringing yourself to the Trinity. It is so that the luminosity of the Trinity may enter like a beam into our soul and get every corner clean, for the luminosity of the Trinity burns, sears deeply.

I am speaking for myself, but I think this applies to every poustinik. I cannot totally desire to bring myself to be thus scorched. Even though I know that the scorching will be done with great love, I don't feel that I want to be scorched. This struggle will repeat itself constantly in the poustinia. God is gentle. He doesn't let us see all the corners of our hearts in one minute.

When I have brought myself to the Trinity and allowed myself to be scorched by his luminosity, I will be able to listen to God. This is a very heavy thing. I find it heavy What it really means is that God now says to me, "Put your roots deep into wisdom This is the moment. I give you the gift of wisdom because the gift is mine but I want it to be given to others. I have ceased to call you my servant. I call you my friend and heir. You are the brother or sister of my Son. So now put your roots deep into wisdom."

Somehow you agree to this, because you have to *agree* to everything. God wants a free lover, a lover who loves freely. He will not push you to do one little thing unless you agree to every bit of it. So the roots go in. Now you begin to *listen* to God. The spirit of discernment comes into you. You begin to understand what God wants, what men want, what you want—the whole shebang!—but mostly what God wants.

Sure, there are moments when you don't want to have these gifts. But they come to you and you accept them because you love God.

11

Kenosis

———————————

The poustinia is a kenotic way of life. By the very fact that you are in the poustinia means that you are tending toward a complete self-emptying. It's something like a steam bath! The whole atmosphere, environment, setting of the poustinia relentlessly reminds you of kenosis. You gradually realize that if you are going to stay in the poustinia, you will have to empty yourself.

This self-emptying has many strata and many dimensions. Its final goal is a holy indifference. These are just two words, but to reach them will take a lifetime.

Emptiness is one aspect of kenosis. It is the constant struggle with one's own imagination, one's own dreams, plans, desires, needs. St. Therese, the Little Flower, gave an example which comes very close to the Russian idea. She said, "I am a little ball. You throw me someplace in a corner. Maybe ten years later you pick me up again." A Russian staretz said that you should be like a rag doll which can be picked up by the hand, foot, or head, thrown in the bushes, now hugged, now thrown in the toy box Two saints had a similar idea.

What does it take to be a ball, a rag doll, having no desire to get up, to move, to do anything that one desires to do? It is something similar to what happens to us when we are told that we have a terminal disease and have only a short time to live. All the things that we have dreamt about, desired, perhaps 98 percent of them fall away in an instant. You are face to face with the stark reality of death, and so your whole life changes in a few minutes. The poustinia is like this. When one is visited by God, a kenosis takes place, and all our plans and projects perish before our eyes.

The desert is an altar on which moment by moment you bring the offering of yourself. For self-will is the obstacle that eternally stands between me and God. We decide that we are going to do such and such a thing. God comes along and says, "No, do this." It's a matter of doing what he wants us to do, not because we are afraid of him, or afraid of dying, but because we are in love with him, and because we enter the poustinia to really do his will and not ours. The poustinia is there to form that attitude in you. The poustinik must finally come to understand that he has to become as empty as his God became for him.

There will come a moment when the offertory procession of man will touch the offertory procession of God. Then man can go anyplace. Then he doesn't need to stay in the poustinia. Then he can pilgrim; he can stop being in one place. He has become so empty that he is simply one who carries God. Now all his ways are straight and plain, ready for the Lord to walk on. It is a strange moment when man realizes by the grace of God that this has taken place in him.

When we hear the parable of the seed, we should think of God becoming a seed in the womb of Mary. He was a good seed. His roots went deep. If ever we can come to dimly understand this strange mystery of God becoming a fetus, a child, a youth, a man, we will begin to understand God's love for us. Then we will begin to understand the emptiness which must take place in us, the depth of surrender of our will to God's. Finally we will come in an offertory procession, and our procession will meet God's procession, and he and we will be one.

This offering of ourselves, if and when it comes, must come from our own freedom. When it comes it will change everything. *Fear* will depart. Whereas before, the poustinik was often beset by many fears, and whereas before, the devil was sniffing all around the poustinia, now it no longer matters because the poustinik knows he has power over the devil.

Where there is kenosis there is no fear. I meditated quite a bit on fear when I lived in Harlem. Was Christ afraid? In Gethsemane he certainly should have been. If he was like us in everything except sin, I can't imagine that he was without fear. He prayed that the chalice would pass from him, but only if it was in accord with his Father's will. You sense some kind of fear there, and you are glad in a way. Glad because he is so very much like us. It makes you feel good. In the same breath, however, we must remember that he got up and went on to Calvary. His fear did not stop his accomplishment of his Father's will.

I remember that when I finished this little meditation in Harlem those many years ago, I ceased to be afraid. I ceased to be afraid because I faced the fact that I might really be killed any day. Perhaps it's when we have accepted the reality of death. like Christ did, that fear ceases and we reach a real depth of kenosis.

With fear, *human respect* also disappears like a vanishing ghost in the night of the desert. Human respect has many faces. We all know very well about the ordinary kind—fear of ridicule. It seems to me there is also a kind of human respect in relation to ourselves. Some of it is wholesome, and some is not. It's wholesome when it acknowledges that everything I have is from God. It is unwholesome when I want to use that which is of God for my own self-aggrandizement.

The poustinia is a fairly stern mother in the beginning. It will gradually wean you, and you have to allow yourself to be weaned from the desire for admiration, adulation, and so on. You will, of course, hear people say that you are this and you are that, that you are holy, that you are wonderful, that you are a "beautiful person." You must develop something akin to what ducks have which allows water to run so easily off their backs! Whenever people say such things, you say quietly in your heart, "If there is anything good in this lecture, this conversation, in my person, it is of you, Lord. All the rest is mine."

This is a very important point. People will accuse you and praise you. You must remain peaceful through both. One of my former spiritual directors, Father Paul Furfey, said to me once: "Catherine, you are a superb lecturer. Now under holy obedience, I want you to forget your lectures. Remember that what's good in them is God's, the rest is yours." In Russia we would call this holy indifference. If people say you are holy, you don't make faces and protest. If people say you are the devil, you don't make faces either. Your heart should be at peace in either case. This, too, is an aspect of kenosis.

Along with fear and human respect, *worrying* also disappears. One of the difficulties of all poustinikki is worrying. It's possible to be introspective in the wrong way, and this leads to worrying. Interiorization is God coming to you; introspection is yourself looking at all those idols that you should be putting on the altar. You spend hours looking at these things when really they should simply be thrown out. Introspection leads you to yourself because it starts with yourself and ends with yourself. Interiorization, on the other hand, starts with God and ends with God. As this latter increases, worrying decreases.

A most excruciating dimension of kenosis has to do with having the courage to speak the word of God. "Open your mouth and I will fill it," says the Lord. If we have no faith that this can happen—or do not have the courage to speak when we are filled—we should keep our mouths closed! An example may help to convey what I mean here.

I had an occasion to lecture to the International Homiletic Society, a society which is concerned with fostering good preaching of the Word. A bishop was the main speaker. For three-quarters of an hour he talked about the importance of study in preparing for a sermon. The more he talked the more uncomfortable I became. I felt positively annihilated, or as the young people would say today, "wiped out." I was praying desperately to God that I would get sick or something so that I wouldn't have to speak. But I knew that God was asking me to speak; he was filling my mouth.

I had to contradict the bishop on almost every point! I talked about the necessity to *pray* before preaching. I received a standing ovation. The bishop was a very humble man. He said: "Catherine, you taught me something. That he who preaches must pray more than he studies." I had to speak, I had to contradict him, because he was wrong, and God was filling my mouth.

So too, a person is led into the poustinia to become empty. This emptiness results in the ability to listen. If the poustinik is attentive and listening in his poustinia, he will also know when he must speak outside the poustinia. They will not be so much his words as the words of Christ. The courage to speak these words is part of the kenosis, part of the emptiness. The words of man suddenly become the Word of God. God takes over, and all our tiny, peanut words suddenly coalesce and in some miraculous way become *The Word*.

The role of the poustinik is allowing himself to quite literally "shut up," to become silent. This means giving up *your* words. Folding the wings of your intellect means giving up the birthplace, the origin, the source of your own words. What for? To become merely dumb, without any speech at all? No. It's in order that *The Word might take over your words*. This is the reason why you are silent in total solitude. It's a strange silence in which you lay your words out on that altar so that you don't have any more of your own words. The birthplace of your own words is now empty. The Russians say, "If you have a recollected and quiet spirit, people will gather around you when you speak." Why is this? Because you won't be speaking; he will.

With this surrender of my words to his Word comes the gift of discernment, the gift of knowing what to say to each person. Because his Word has taken over my words, a clarity enters into me which enables me to see the heart of the other and to know what to say. When we are surrendered to his Word, the gift of discernment will make our words quite flexible. Now compassionate, now merciful, now most direct—the clarity which his Word has brought and which I have accepted at great pain to myself now goes out as a ray of light to somebody else.

If you wish, this is one of the *charisms* of the poustinia.

It's an excruciating charism because one of the differences between me and all creatures in the world is my speech, the ability to talk. The poustinik must learn to speak anew, out of his heart, the words God gives him. It's like learning to talk all over again.

Thus kenosis is the process whereby a novice is changed into a staretz. This is not a matter of chronological age. Youth changes into wisdom. You become wise when you become empty. The world finds it difficult to accept emptiness. "Nature," it is said, "abhors a vacuum." It is the same in the world of the spirit. Your emptiness is filled now with God, with the Trinity.

Kenosis in the beginning seems to tire you out. Eventually it becomes tireless, effortless. Your kenosis is filled with Christ, Christ the preacher, who answers endless questions during the day, and Christ the pray-er, who goes away to pray in the night. The kenosis has to be there in the poustinia. It is the fierce and terrible struggle between your desires to direct and arrange your life, and God's will. Such a battle will tire you indeed. But when you begin to move into the world you will be tireless. You will be tireless as you go on Christ's mission, tireless as you answer questions, tireless as you travel to all sorts of strange places. This tirelessness is the gift of the poustinia. God enticed you there to make you tireless for him. The words become The Word. Weakness becomes strength. These things will happen as a result of your constant going to the altar and laying on it things great and small. Then, one day, by his grace, by his goodness, you will lie upon it yourself.

Kenosis, you might say, is the basic core idea of Russian spirituality. For the poustinik, the most powerful of all his thoughts and prayers should be to empty himself as Christ emptied himself by his Incarnation. We will never reach that depth, but that is the poustinik's vocation.

Kenosis for the poustinik is first of all a hidden reality. I had a painter friend who restored things. There is a compound which you put over a picture. You let it dry for a while, then you cover it with another kind of chemical. When that dries it becomes like a film over the picture which, when removed, restores the picture in all its vivid colors. I sometimes think of kenosis in that way. It's like peeling a dirty film from our lives, a camouflage self, to reveal beneath the skin a true child of God.

We are like children playing with Plasticine figurines which we have fashioned for ourselves, for our amusement. Then, not like children, we adore them. Possessions become idols in this way. The hands of a poustinik are always to be empty. He uses things for his health, for his needs, to be able to help others, but nothing sticks to his fingers, but I mean the fingers of his mind and heart. It's awfully difficult to let go of this "I" that appears to us to be the essence of ourselves. To us it is unthinkable to surrender this self. Yet we must.

We must surrender our intellect and will in the natural order of things. When we detach ourselves from these we seem for a while as if we're totally bereft of our personality. Actually, what we have done is hand them over to God. The Russian word for "purgatory" is close to the English word for "laundry." We hand our mind and will over to God to be laundered, to be washed. True, they have been cleansed in Baptism, but we are not always faithful to our baptismal rebirth. By kenosis they are washed by Christ through the Spirit's gifts of discernment and wisdom.

How are our minds and hearts washed by Christ? The only way I can describe it is to say that they are cleansed as we pass through some experience of nothingness. There are periodic moments in which you are as if dead. There are certain moments in your prayers or thinking—moments in your life with God—when suddenly you *mean* what you are saying or doing with all your heart and soul, with everything that you are. At those moments you are saying in effect, "Take my mind and my will, Lord, and cleanse them." At these times you really *mean it*. Do these moments last a minute, an hour, a day? You don't know. You only know that afterwards, your mind and your will have been returned to you cleansed. You are more alive.

To elaborate a bit more on this point, perhaps I could use the example of Sartre again.

I was asked to lecture on Sartre once. To prepare for my talk I began reading some of his works. As I was reading I got very tired. I sat down on the bed. I said to myself: "Sartre leads you to nonbeing. Isn't that what Christ also calls us to? Isn't that what the mystics write about? Yes," I said to myself, "but Christ leads us not to negation but to surrender. Christ leads only to a seeming negation which is actually the heights of the mountain. Sartre leads us to a nothingness which is *really nothing*, the bottom of a pit." All I can say is that our minds and wills are cleansed when we allow Christ to lead us through nothingness to the heights of the mountain. Before that moment arrives there will be a terrible amount of willpower exercised in our prayer, our retreats, and our returns. But at some point they will be cleansed. This is no joke. This is a real fight. This is the desert.

Now we are able to discern the will of God. Our senses are acute, attuned, because we are listening to God. We are able to make wise decisions because of our discernment. Because we have surrendered our minds and wills to God, they are given back to us: We receive back, as it were, our own gifts. This is the first step in following Christ—this smashing of the idol of oneself.

The prospect of this kenosis will frighten us because we are so cowardly. Who isn't afraid? So it is better to ask Our Lady to take hold of that corner of the film as it is pulled off. One does not really know how a painting feels when a film is removed from it. But we have some idea what it's like to remove the film from our false selves. 'It's like peeling some skin off our bodies: it hurts. So we should call upon Mary's gentle hand to help us remove this film from our lives. This is the hidden process, the first step of kenosis. It is hidden between God and us. It is a giving up of one's will and oneself into the hands of God.

Kenosis cannot happen without our cooperation. There are moments when we wish that God hadn't given us freedom so we wouldn't have to choose. But he isn't going to remove our freedom. He's not going to *make us* do anything. Like all the virtues, this kenosis, this surrender, this emptying, must come as a result of our cooperation.

Kenosis demands a kind of death, and this dying will draw attacks from the enemy, from Satan; but it will always draw forth new graces, new charisms from God. We will be—not in the eye of the hurricane, with the hurricane storming all around us—we will be *in the hurricane*. We will be buffeted until we are almost exhausted, until we are ready to give in. We will be on the point of saying, "This kenosis business is no good, it's asking too much, it's impossible." This is a very critical moment, because just as I am about to rationalize the whole thing away, the emptying comes. All I have to say is *credo*, and then cry out with all my heart, "See, Lord, out of the depths I cry to thee; out of the depths where I am besieged by devils and by the idols of my own mind; out of the depths of the freedom you have given me, I cry to thee. Liberate me. Make me free to empty myself."

This point is not reached without a great deal of difficulty, fighting with ourselves, fighting with Satan. But this is the critical moment when symbolic hands slowly open the door wide enough to throw out all that shouldn't be in you, to let in all that should be there. The moment of kenosis is approaching.

Discernment reaches a new stage of perfection. It blossoms like a beautiful flower. You discern that you are entering into the mystery of the Incarnation. For what did Christ do but empty himself by taking on flesh in the womb of the Virgin? Now you are in the same position he was. He emptied himself to take upon himself the sin of mankind. He emptied himself so that he could atone before the Father for all that needed redemption. He reopened the doors of paradise for men.

Kenosis leads one to that reality of the Incarnation. Why enter into this kenosis? "In order," as St. Paul says, "to make up for what is wanting in the sufferings of Christ on behalf of his body, which is the church." In order to share in the sufferings of Christ. This is the whole aim and goal of kenosis. This is where it leads. It is not done for any selfish reason. It is not even done to be "one with God." We must go beyond such motivation and take upon ourselves the pain of humanity. Unless we can do that, we will not be able to place the gift of our kenosis into the hands of God. Kenosis, like everything else, is primarily for the other.

Such steps are only the beginning. This emptying of self must continue. This contact with God has to be maintained constantly; the carrying of man's pain and sorrow and joy has to go on unceasingly. Otherwise there will be breaks and gaps in our relationship with God. This cannot be allowed to happen, once we have started on this journey. The going will be rough, but the joy too will be ineffable. The poustinik will eventually realize that this is the whole reason why he has come into the poustinia. He becomes a fool for God because God became a fool for him. He comes to understand how the foolishness of God is true wisdom.

Every Christian should be living this kenotic way of life. But the second part which I have described—the entrance into the mystery of the Incarnation—cannot happen without the first, the hidden stripping of self. What follows is a lifetime of continued stripping, of emptying oneself and becoming a nonentity. You remain, free, easy, direct, but especially simple. "Learn of me because I am meek and humble of heart." Simplicity is the very essence of kenosis.

Part III

Words from the Poustinia

12

Touching God

As I have explained to you before, when a Russian goes into a poustinia, he goes for others as well as for himself— but predominantly for others. Upon returning, he should tell members of his family or community what he has received during his stay in the poustinia. If one were in a Russian village, these words would be meant for everyone in the village. I do this at the community in Madonna House. I either catch them at supper, or later on in the day which follows my poustinia. I bow before them and say, "May the peace of the Blessed Trinity be with you," or something similar, and they answer, "And also with you." I then share with them a word from the Lord.

Someone may ask, "How do you hear this 'word of the Lord'?" Let me explain.

It is understood that since the reason for entering the poustinia is one of listening to God in prayer and fasting, the first act of a poustinik is to fold the wings of his intellect and open the doors of his heart. The Russians would say: Put your head into your heart and try to achieve a deep and profound interior silence. It is then, when one is deeply silent, that God begins to speak.

When I say "God begins to speak," I mean that the

mind is purified, the heart is at peace, and out of the depths
of both come forth the gifts or the fruits of the Holy Spirit.
Quietly, imperceptibly, out of this overshadowing of the
Holy Spirit comes a word, a thought, a sentence, as the
case may be.

Someone might say, "All this sounds very mystical."
There is a difference between what the East means by
mystical and what the West means. I think the East would
call normal many things that the West might term mystical.
If you are in the poustinia and God knocks on your door
and speaks to you, that doesn't sound mystical to me; it
sounds quite normal. He said he would speak to us. Many
Westerners may believe that they are not worthy that God
should speak to them thus. Of course we are not worthy!
If for one minute you think that you are worthy that God
should speak to you in the poustinia, you should get out of
the poustinia! It is because we are not worthy that we can
say, "How wonderful God is, he comes and speaks to
unworthy me!" You can't pay any attention to whether
you are worthy or not. Everybody is unworthy—but still
God speaks to us.

So it is common around Madonna House for someone
to ask a person coming out of the poustinia to the
community, "What has the Lord said to you?" implying,
"What has he said to you *for us?*"

It seems that it is a little difficult for people to tell us
what they have received in the poustinia. For those who
only stay for 24 hours, it takes a long time to get used to
listening to God and sharing what he has said. But poustinikki who are in the poustinia for a long time should be
able to tell once in a while what God has told them. Because they are there for us, for others. They are there to
share. It's very important. It takes the guts out of you

to share, because God touched you. Listening is touching. Smelling is touching. We don't want to share it with others. But if we don't we'll never hear it again. What you hear is part of the Good News, in a sense, a word of God (I hope I'm not heretical in this!). There is something of the Lord in it, and you are meant to share it.

Such a sharing is not always easy. A word comes to you and you know, deep down, in quiet prayer, that you have to share it. You suddenly know that you have to say this thing, and you don't want to. You say, "I don't want to! I don't want to! I don't want to!" But then, if you refuse God, if you refuse to pass on something that is being said to you, you can't sleep, you can't eat, you can't do anything. You might just as well be dead. It's going to come out, that's all there is to it. When it does come out, then you can relax. It's almost as if the word were torn out of you. This, to my mind, is what prophecy is. In this section, I would like to share with you some of these "words from the poustinia."

One of the favorite images I like to use for describing the Christian life is of a person standing with arms outstretched. One hand, in faith and prayer, touches God; the other hand is extended in service to the neighbor. Thus is a person cruciform, touching God and touching neighbor. It seemed that the words which came to me in the poustinia revolved around these two themes.

Faith

It is evening. In fact, it is already quarter past seven. Today was a very strange day in the poustinia. I must admit that throughout the day nothing made sense to me. Perhaps it was because I was very tired and just wanted to lie down in the sun, read a few spiritual books, and an excerpt or two from the bible. This I did.

I listened to God through all this haze but no special word seemed to come through. It seemed to me as if I were suspended betwixt and between whatever place God suspends people. It seemed as if he said, "Rest," so I rested. I must admit it was lovely. The sun was shining and I relaxed. I swam in the river and rested some more; I slept a little.

Time marched on and toward seven o'clock, slowly, very slowly, a word began forming itself.

It was a strange word, a big word. A word I didn't expect at all. The word was *faith!* Confronted with this word, for some reason or other, I was like one dumb (or bereft of all my senses would perhaps be a better description). Or maybe I was like one asleep who wasn't reacting.

Why I felt that way I don't know, because I use the word faith constantly! But this time it seemed to stand out in another context. I looked at faith with clear eyes, with deep eyes, and I once again realized with a depth I had never experienced before, that faith is a gift of God.

This realization came suddenly, and with it a sort of fullness of understanding that it is a pure gift indeed, and that God alone can bestow it. At the same time I realized that God passionately desires to give it to us. I realized that he wanted us to ask for it, for he only could give it to us when we asked for it (that is, of course, after his original gift to us in Baptism).

It seems that when we ask for faith we are, as it were, turning our face toward his face, for we have to! It seems in truth that God desires this very simple action to happen so that he can face us, face to face! Yes, he wants to look at our face. He loves to see our face facing him, for so often we avoid this simple act. Even while we beg him for simple favors we somehow close not only our physical eyes but the eyes of our souls as well—strangely avoiding looking at him. Yet we know that he always looks at us, looks at us with deep love.

Faith, that God-given gift that had healed so many of those who believed in God even long before Baptism came or was instituted as a sacrament by Jesus Christ. There were the leper, the blind man, the woman with the issue of blood, the servant of the Roman soldier, and millions of others who are not mentioned in any recorded documents. For there were thousands upon thousands I am sure who were healed through whatever faith in a Supreme Being they had during the history of man's living and believing.

Faith is the father of love and of hope, as well as of trust and confidence. Faith sees God's face in every human face. Faith, as it slowly grows, and as we pray for it and beseech God for it, identifies us with Christ.

Faith allows us to enter peacefully into the dark night which faces every one of us at one time or another. Faith is at peace, and full of light. Faith celebrates the very warp and woof of one's existence. Faith considers that its precariousness and its finiteness are but the womb in which it abides, moving toward the plentitude and fullness of the eternity which it desires and believes in and which revelation opens to it.

Faith walks simply, childlike, between the darkness of human life and the hope of what is to come. "For eye has not seen, nor ear heard what God reserves for those who love him." Faith is fundamentally a kind of folly, I guess, the folly that belongs to God himself.

Faith, I repeat, is the father of love and hope, of trust and confidence. Faith heals by asking God to heal. Faith heals others because of the faith I have in the Lord. Faith is an incredible, fantastic reality, untouchable, unweighable, yet visible and real. Faith is a contact between God and man.

Man's face is turned to God through faith, and their eyes meet, so that every day becomes more and more luminous. The veil between God and man becomes less and less until it seems that man can almost reach out and touch God. Faith breaks through barriers. Faith makes love into a bonfire. Faith holds the wind of the Holy Spirit which fans the bonfire into flame. Faith thrusts its hands into the hands of the martyr and so brings the martyr to his knees. Faith is contagious when we show it to one another. Men cannot resist faith even when they deny it and laugh at it and jeer at it and even kill the one who has faith. Killing those who believe is simply multiplying belief, for the blood of martyrs is the seed of faith!

What about us? What about us men and women of today? We certainly must pray for faith, especially we who desire to preach the gospel with our lives. Without faith we cannot do it. We must believe in God. We must believe in our fellowman. We must enter into trust and confidence with quiet steps but without hesitation, without cerebration. Truly here is the moment of the heart, not of the head. The head will rationalize, will turn its face away from faith, from love, from hope, from confidence. The head will put its hand behind its back so as not to touch the martyr, the prostitute, the publican.

Few men go where no one wants to go. If we have faith in God we must have faith in men. Even the most evil among us has some redeeming feature. Faith will seek it out.

It is so important for us to have faith, trust, confidence in one another. It is the only way we can communicate.

Without faith there is no communication, there is no love, or if there was a little love it will die without hope, trust, and confidence. Even if it doesn't die right away, it will be so ill, so weak, and so tired that communication will be miserable as well.

Faith alone can restore communication. Yes, it is time we should believe in one another. It is time we should return to God and ask to be healed from this strange lack of faith, this strange lack of confidence and trust in one another. This is the moment, this is the hour to turn our face to God and ask to be healed from the fear of trusting, from the fear of confiding, from the fear of believing in one another.

"Lord, behold, we are all kneeling here together, beseeching you to give us an increase of faith. Let our hearts be open to you. Let our heads be put into our hearts. Let faith, hope, love, trust, confidence reign among us. Let us be done with human respect. Let us be done with being afraid of ridicule. Let us be done with thinking we have to hide anything from one another. Lord, behold, we are in need of healing. Maranatha—Come, Lord, we need you so."

Defenselessness and Forgiveness

For the last few days, for some unaccountable reason, I have been thinking about defenselessness and forgiveness. These two thoughts have wended their way into my heart and mind off and on for quite a while now. As usual, I wondered from whence such words came to me, but then I smiled, remembering that for years now I had ceased to wonder about the words that came through my mind and heart.

I must be truthful: I was afraid to examine these words

in depth. Defenselessness, especially, is a frightening word! It means to be without defense or without protection. I realized at once that it had nothing to do with physical defenselessness, namely, the lack of being armed with some weapon. No, that was not the meaning of this word that was knocking at the door of my heart to be let out. Defenselessness had something to do with the will of God and with a sort of total freedom that he wanted through that defenselessness.

Yes, it had something to do with some new dimension in the Lord, as if he wanted to say to me, "Come higher unto my mountain and listen to what I want to tell you." I must admit that I didn't want to go any higher unto any mountain. Yet, when I say this I feel that I am a liar, because the inner and outward voice of God for me, even disguised in my own thoughts, has been always too powerful to resist.

I said to myself, "Well, it's good to live according to the will of God, because that defenselessness must be hidden somewhere in the will of God. Otherwise, why should I become defenseless?" My thoughts went back and forth, so I prayed for a moment and looked up my friend Staretz Silouan in the book that I like so much—*The Undistorted Image*. There I read the following: "It is a great good to give oneself up to the will of God. The Lord alone is in the soul. No other thought can enter in and the soul feels God's love even though the body is suffering."

I had known this truth for a long time, but today in the poustinia I also asked myself how in truth did I live out the will of God to achieve that freedom that I knew all along is somewhere deeply contained in that will?

Once more I turned to *The Undistorted Image* (p. 157): "He who lives according to God's will has this sign to go by: If you are distressed over anything, it means that you are not fully surrendered to God's will, although it may seem to you that you live according to his will. He who lives according to God's will has no cares. If he has need of something, he offers himself and the thing he wants to God, and if he does not receive it he remains as tranquil as if he had got what he wanted."

Well, that made sense to me, because if I were really given over to the will of God totally, then I would fear nothing, and I would be totally free. I wouldn't need any defenses, any weapons, any psychological coping devices. What for? In everything that happened to me I would say: "Such is God's pleasure." I would accept whatever comes to me with joy.

My thoughts turned to death at this moment. Man fundamentally fears death above everything else. He fears dissolution. But with this defenselessness that leads to total freedom there would be no fear, no defenses against even death. And I looked back upon my life. True, the Lord put me through a little novitiate of defenselessness. For I have been persecuted. I have been ill. I have lived in great poverty for quite a while. Looking back I saw that I was defenseless, or tried to be. I also saw that I failed sometimes, and put up little defenses against people who tried to persecute me.

But now I understood that God wanted me to give up even these defenses—all of them. Defenselessness against death, defenselessness against people. defenselessness against everything—for defenselessness was holy. It gave you total freedom. The soul then would truly walk in the footsteps of Christ who was led like a lamb to the slaughter and accepted it all, including death. Then the person would experience resurrection right here and now.

He would have the freedom of the children of God. He would really know that God has ceased to call him a servant and now calls him his friend!

Oh, what an immense and holy knowledge would come to this person! I beheld the periphery of that knowledge in my poustinia, and yet I knew that somehow or other I had to use yet another key to understand it in its fullness. Again I prayed to God to enlighten me. I prayed to the Most Holy Trinity, to the Holy Spirit, for it was the Father who gave me this Holy Spirit to enlighten me. At this moment of prayer I suddenly understood that before I really could become free in that total defenselessness that is ready to do the will of God in utter simplicity—in the depths and heights shown by him—I must forgive!

Then an immense panorama, an immense view, beautiful and serene, unrolled itself before my eyes. I understood that not only do I have to forgive all my enemies, but I had to do more—I had to love them, love them with the love of Christ. For hadn't he said, "By this shall men know you are my disciples, that you love one another as I have loved you"? But how could I love with the love of Christ? How could I become so utterly defenseless as to allow that love to flourish within me, watered by the waters of forgiveness? How could I achieve this freedom that this defenselessness and forgiveness would give me. Again I prayed to the Most Holy Trinity and the answer came to me in one word: faith.

Yes, I had to not only believe in what I always believed, namely, forgiveness, loving my enemies. But this time I had to enter into deep faith, holding hands with defenselessness and forgiveness, that is to say, becoming myself defenseless and forgiving. It is love that will make me forgive always and every time! So I began to meditate on

the power of love. Once again I experienced a return to the
Holy Land, where I had an encounter with Christ. Having
experienced *him*, I lost all interest in the places where he
was, where he lived, and which he visited.

This time in my poustinia my encounter with him was
different. I simply contemplated his incarnation, his birth,
his life in Nazareth, his preaching years, his passion. I heard
him, as it were, very clearly, forgiving all his enemies from
the height of his cross. Then a great chorus sounded, the
chorus of all those who followed his footsteps, from
Stephen the first martyr, to St. Sebastian, to a whole crowd
of people who in one way or another died a martyr's death
and kept forgiving those who hurt them and brought them
to this death.

Yet, each one of these could have escaped in one way
or another. They could have given incense to gods with a
mental reservation, but none of them did. All of them
were defenseless. They all walked in the footsteps of the
Lamb, led to the slaughter because of love of him. This
is when I began to really understand what defenselessness
means, because I began to understand what forgiveness
means.

Forgiveness means the incarnation of God's words to
his apostles. The incarnation of the command that we
love one another as he loved us. I also knew that God
himself would now teach us about the depths and the
heights of this defenselessness and this forgiveness, for he
alone could. Yes, God himself will teach me and all of
us who want to enter this new dimension of his heart, his
holy mountain.

This realization brought a tremendous joy to me which
I share with you. By becoming our teacher he also makes
us realize with a tremendous clarity that he considers us

his friends and will talk to us as to his friends. Yes, the more I meditated on trying to be defenseless and forgiving, the more I understood what this true freedom of Christ meant.

God's love is insatiable. He wants us to go into the depths of his heart. But his heart is fathomless. Our defenselessness means to do his will. To do his will means to enter into this heart of his, this insatiable, loving heart that died for us and was wounded by a lance. It means to forgive all enemies, great or small. It means to be his reflection. To forgive everyone who in the smallest way upset or hurt us is to be a reflection of his loving heart. So to be defenseless and to forgive is to be free. Now nothing can touch us. We are indeed in God and God is in us. Alleluia!

Now the Holy Spirit fills us with a constantly growing love of the Trinity. Now we understand a little better why he too was defenseless and why he forgave, for through those attitudes of the heart Love came to dwell among us. If we follow him, and understand those two words with our hearts, defenselessness and forgiveness will fill the earth.

Listening

The word which came to me today in the poustinia was listening. I had meditated on this word quite a bit in the past, but it had never come to me so directly, so vividly, so poignantly as it did today. I really had to take it into my heart and meditate on it in depth. While I was considering it, this poem came to mind:

> Listen to yourself so as to find the path
> to God within the frail walls of your humanness.

Listen to yourself, for it is you alone who
will lead yourself to him, or away from him.
Listen to yourself, listen to God, when you
have led yourself to him.
Listen well, for if you hear his voice you
will be wise with the wisdom of the Lord,
and then you will be able to hear the voice
of men, not as a surging sea, or as a mob.
But each man's speech is his own, a treasure
given to you beyond all expectations, because you led yourself to him and listened
to his voice.

I wrote that poem down immediately and when I had
finished I was a little bewildered!

I didn't quite understand it. I had to meditate upon
it again and again. Slowly, very slowly, it began to make
sense. It meant a journey inward again. A journey inward
that would take will power to accomplish. That is to say,
I would have to use that will power under duress, pushing
myself into it instead of walking easily. Yes, I had to
force myself onto that journey inward, even though I was
reluctant to go. I realized that the journey inward was a
confrontation with the Trinity that dwells within me.

Strange, that listening had something to do with the
Trinity. Strange, that I had to lead myself there of my own
free will. Maybe to you this is all very clear, but it wasn't
for me. So, during this poustinia, I undertook to lead
myself to the Trinity on that eternal journey inward, the
journey that man must undertake to find the God who
dwells therein.

At this time, the urge, the need, as it were, was very
direct and very powerful. The call was there. I had to
answer it. Nevertheless, I was free to undertake the jour-

ney inward or not to undertake it. I could answer the call
or I could reject it.

So, in this poustinia, I really battled and struggled with
God. I struggled because for some unaccountable reason
I did not want to go. It seemed a little bit frightening.
Can you imagine that it can be frightening? Well, as far
as I was concerned, it was. So I fought. It was a day of
struggling and fighting with the Lord. I got tired, so I
slept.

I slept and woke up again—and struggled again. But
finally I took the journey. It seemed as if I came to the
Trinity. What does it mean to come to the Trinity? To
me it means to come into the light from a very great darkness. It means to come into peace from a great turmoil.
It means to come into joy from a painful and joyless journey. When I came before the Trinity (which appeared as
all motion and light), I fell asleep again!

Suddenly I woke up and listened to myself. I don't
know how I got the grace to listen to myself, but I did. It
was as if all the corners of my person were illuminated,
and I clearly saw much in me that wanted to talk to me
and that I wanted to talk to. As the dialogue took place
I discovered that it was really the grace of loving myself!

You cannot really love your neighbor unless you love
yourself first. The Lord said, "Love your neighbor *as
yourself*." In a strange luminosity of the Trinity I realized
that I had to love myself more than I did because God
loved me. I found this out by listening to myself. I grew
in reverence, love, and adoration of the God who created
me and dwelt within me.

I realized too that loving one's self included also loving
God who dwells within me. It becomes interwoven, this
love affair, like a piece of weaving. The warp and woof

blend in some strange and uncanny way. Then I realized in depth that I was an icon of Christ.

But I saw more, and I saw with a clarity that was incredible. I saw that I was an heir to my Father's love and, to all his goods. I saw that I was a sister to Christ, and that I indeed always walked in the shadow of the wings of the Holy Spirit. These realities apply to all of us who know how to listen. The gift of listening is part of the gift of wisdom for which we pray, and for which I had prayed intensely at that moment.

Again I slept and awoke. This time I understood that now for some unaccountable reason (or perhaps accountable) I could, should, and would listen to men. They would come to me not as a mob, not as a raging sea, not as a group, but individually, one by one. I realized that the roots of listening must be planted in the soil of wisdom, for only from that soil would the depth of reverence come with which we could listen to one another.

I also understood the totality of my gift. For when we listen to one another we must be totally surrendered to the person, totally attentive to his speech. Also, we must be totally dependent on God for our replies. I don't know if I am theologically correct, but at that moment I thought of the Holy Spirit as one who listens to each of us and dispenses his gifts to each one of us. I also understood that this listening of the Holy Spirit is so profound, so immense, that no one can probe it. Yet, I thought that we must strive toward that immensity, toward that profundity.

Somehow (I know this sounds crazy), I thought that in a sense, while I was listening, I disappeared! Only a heart remained, and in that heart the Holy Spirit listened instead of me. Yet I was a part of it. The Holy Spirit imparted to me that to which I had to listen, clearing the road of all indecisiveness, of all stuttering, and this seemed to me to be the moment in which the Holy Spirit gives the gift of discernment.

Perhaps I should have spoken first of the ability to listen to God after I had listened to myself. But in a sense it doesn't matter, because this word listening that came to me in the poustinia was a combination of all these things. Listening to myself, listening to God, listening to men—all blended into one word—love!

Listening to God has a dreamlike quality. Oh, you are awake. But you are at work. It is an interiorized situation in which he comes to you and clears a little bit of your heart. He makes it comfortable there for himself and there he talks to you as a friend to a friend. You feel as if you are sitting at his feet like Mary, listening, just listening. It is as if God came to prepare you again and again to listen to men. At this moment the Holy Spirit enters with a great strength and vigor and suddenly the gift of wisdom and discernment becomes like a huge shady tree that grows from your heart, inviting people to sit under it and rest.

With the gift of listening comes the gift of healing, because listening to your brother until he has said the last word in his heart is healing and consoling. Someone has said that it is possible "to listen a person's soul into existence." I like that.

One point that came to me strongly during this strange day of struggling was that all these gifts demand the annihilation of self. One cannot intrude oneself while listening to another. Truly, here the wings of the intellect are folded only to be unfolded by the Holy Spirit who alone knows when this immense gift from God, the intellect, must be used to help the one to whom we are listening. Always the essence of the listener is one of deep reverence, infinite respect, and deep gratitude to God for having selected us for that listening.

Yes, it is a deep and profound thing that I fought through and delved into here in the poustinia. There is more, but I am tired. I know that the Lord will give me words to tell you about what follows, for it is he who has given me the word listening. If he so desires, he will give me the next word, or a fuller explanation of this same one.

Transparency

The word which was coming to me on this occasion was *transparency*. We must take such a word and unwrap it, and begin to think about and pray about it.

What I mean by thinking and praying about it is again a sort of stillness of the heart that allows whatever word the Holy Spirit gives to really mature and blossom within oneself. So, in this way, the word transparency took hold of me as the other words had done, and I knew that I would have to examine it carefully on my knees in the poustinia.

I must admit it was hard going. For some unaccountable reason this word eluded me. I prayed and kept my soul in patience and, I hope, in serenity and tranquillity, awaiting the coming of the Spirit to clarify it for me. The Lord said that the Spirit would be sent to us by the Father so that he might clarify for us all the things that Jesus told us.

Thus meditating, I fell asleep for about an hour or so. I woke up refreshed, and the word transparency took possession of me. I cried out to the Lord, "Lord, how are these words coming to me, and why are they coming to me? Do you really send them to me? They are so strange."

What is transparency? I see a window washed clean,

through which whatever light is outside comes in, as if there were no window at all. For the window is so well washed, so transparent, that it ceases to be glass, and blends, or seems to, with the air around it. If there is sun outside such a window, it floods the room with its golden light, obliterating the window completely, because of its transparency.

Is transparency the window you desire to make out of men who love you or try to? In our polluted, opaque world there are few ordinary windows which can be washed clean. Even if they could be washed clean, there is little light and sunshine that can seep through them. We have polluted the air to such an extent that any light, even sunlight, barely reaches the earth.

Is the word transparency your answer to our polluted world, our polluted minds, hearts and souls? It may be, because if we unpollute our inner selves, then of course we will be selfless, and if we are selfless we easily will unpollute the air, the water, the earth, because selfless men in love with God are not subject to greed, and it is greed that today pollutes the earth. But greed pollutes the inner man before it pollutes the earth.

Is this your way to unpollute the world? I repeat. For if the soul itself, the person, was truly defenseless, forgiving, and loving, the result of this would be transparent minds, hearts and souls. A transparent soul would show *you* to everyone who seeks you, for unless we become transparent, people will not know you. For every human face is also the icon of Christ—so is every human heart. But for the icon to be reflected in the face, it must be painted in the hearts of men.

To achieve such transparency means again answering Christ's call—"Friend, come higher." To go higher in this case means to cry out to the Holy Spirit, for only his gifts and his fruits can help us to achieve such a transparency. Calling to the Holy Spirit! Is this why the charismatic movement has got hold of so many people across the world? Is this why the faces of men have been turned toward the Holy Spirit, our Advocate, so that we might implore him to make us transparent by washing us clean in his fire and water? So that we might offer our transparency as the gift of the Holy Spirit to a world searching desperately for you?

One of the gifts of the Holy Spirit is the gift of tears. We must then implore him to give us this gift of tears, for it is only with tears of love and compunction that we will be able to wash the windows of our soul and place in it, brilliantly lighted, the signposts you have left us which are yourself. For you are the signpost that shows us the way to the Father, so that we may know you, the Triune God.

Yes, I think I have grasped a little the outlines of this immense word, transparency, which also means a total opening to others. Transparency is that through which we begin to unpollute all pollution, especially of the Church, of modern Christians so mired in the opaqueness of modern theologians' excesses.

So, transparency is given us that all Christians, whatever position they might be in, will become unpolluted in deed and in truth. Yes, that we might become united, of one mind, in the unity of the Father, Son, and Holy Spirit. Is this what you mean by transparency, Lord? I think you did, so this is the word I bring to you, my friends.

Poverty

It is again one of those strange days in my poustinia, a kind of day that happens so often lately. Perhaps I could call it a "depression day," for it seems depressive, and yet, I don't think it is. Depressions rarely come to those who try to pray. No, it isn't a depression. It's a sort of "cosmic sadness."

I asked myself again and again, "What is a cosmic sadness?" The answer came quite simply: It is the feeling resulting from the sight Christ saw in the garden of Gethsemane where perhaps he realized that his sacrifice would be in vain for so many people. Out of his humanity came that cry to his Father to allow this chalice to pass him by. That seemed to be "cosmic sadness" as I felt it then.

But another element entered into this poustinia. I really saw that I wanted to escape from it, for in it, in this element, I had to face God so often. For some unaccountable reason this Friday of all other Fridays I seemed to be either in awe of him or afraid of him; maybe I was afraid of the pain to which his love was eternally calling me. It wasn't until about quarter past four or thereabouts that the word came to me. It was *poverty!*

Yes, poverty just won't let me be. I remembered St. Francis who used to call poverty his Lady Fair. But to me, poverty is more like a sister, a twin sister who walks where I walk, eats where I eat, sleeps where I sleep. Today poverty was connected with purity of heart.

A sentence was clearly forming within my heart: purity of heart is the love of those who fall again and again—the sinners—it is love of the humble, the simple, the humiliati.

This is a rather simple sentence, yet very profound, and which sort of baffles me when I think about it. *Purity of heart is love for the weak who constantly fall.* Yes, this is as close as I can come to this strange sentence. Let me repeat it again: Purity of heart is love for the weak who fall, and who is not weak?

Looking out of the window of my poustinia I suddenly saw how tenderly, how gently, how warmly, how lovingly Christ bends toward the world. At that moment I also understood the words "cosmic charity," and when these words touched me, they expanded my heart to embrace especially all those who are weak and who keep on falling.

But then I looked again and I realized that everyone is weak and everyone falls! Does that mean that to be pure of heart one must love everyone? From the very depth of my soul came the answer, "Yes." That is what is meant by being pure of heart. Now I began to understand why the pure of heart will see God. It is because God has come to heal and to restore, and it is the weak who need healing. I have to open my heart to everyone who is weak, and that means *everyone*. Now I know why the pure of heart shall see God, and even see him now, *because he is in the ones who are weak*.

Yes, he will be in them, in each one of them, and that thought brought me to the sacrifice of the Eucharist. I saw the bread given to everyone present and I realized vividly and clearly that everyone among those present, including myself, was weak, prone to the failing and falling again and again, and somehow I understood with the heart what the beatitude meant. I understood too that the kingdom of God begins now. So does the "sight" of God begin now for those who are pure of heart.

At this sight the heart must truly enlarge itself. Now I understood why I myself felt so terribly poor when I considered the pain of the world. For it was my turn to pass through Gethsemane as Christ did. Yes, I had to pass through Gethsemane with the full, clear vision of what it means to be a Christian, another Christ, to be crucified and lifted up. Yes, I understood what it meant to be pure of heart and to see God, but what did purity of heart have to do with poverty?

As I pondered over this a sentence from the Fathers seemed to come floating through the air. "If you see your brother in the act of sinning, throw the cloak of your love over his shoulder."

If this is true, if that is the way we are to understand purity of heart as the ability to love as he loved, then I began to understand how all pertained to poverty. For as the heart becomes pure, as it is enlarged by the Lord, as it is ready to go to Gethsemane, as it finally sees in the weak and in those who fall the face of God, its gaze also turns in upon itself and begins to see what it itself is made of before the face of God. Here, I think, is where poverty entered my contemplation.

Unless I know myself, none of this purity of heart can take root in me. The poverty I speak of which comes through the understanding of myself and others is the fruit of love—the immense, incredible love that comes to all those who allow themselves to be pure of heart, that is, purified by God himself. *To allow this to happen means to enter the abyss of poverty!*

Now I have truly opened my door, the door of my heart, to him who knocked at it so long. Now I have let him in and I have said to him, "Lord, this is your home. Please take out of it anything you don't like. Make my heart not only a place for you to live in, but also a place for you to rest in. For behold, Lord, I have loved you since I remember myself, but my heart has acquired, as every one of us does, so many things. Take them away! My heart and everything that is in it are all yours, for in opening my door to you I surrender myself to you."

Yes, I did surrender to him, which to me simply meant

that I surrendered my person with a totality which I never thought possible before. In doing so I found true poverty.

Whenever the Lord enters, all other things simply disappear. It is as if God took the furnishings of my heart and threw them away. But he didn't move, he didn't act. He simply looked around and they vanished. That is the way he acted when sick people were brought to him. As with the leper, he cured by simply looking.

Now in truth, on this day in August, I rested naked before the Lord, naked of heart that is. Then it seemed that suddenly a sort of fog lifted from my face, a fog that had been there for so long. I looked at every member of the community and I saw them as perhaps God was seeing them from my empty heart. I looked again and saw all those who passed through Madonna House, people whose names I didn't remember but whose faces I often do. In each I saw God's face and realized that in doing so I was being purified. Purity of heart!

Still, dimly and gropingly, I suddenly understood that the realization of poverty, coupled with the raging, flaming desire to see God, was burning me up. Today in the poustinia I somehow incredibly discovered how and why the pure of heart see God. Yes, I think I did. Amen.

Com-Passion

The word that comes to me today is compassion, but in my mind—or is it my heart?—it is spelled com-passion. For quite a while I sat very quietly contemplating this word. There are moments in the poustinia when an intense stillness surrounds me, and it is in this stillness that the word that comes to me flowers. Still, I wondered, what did it mean? Where was *this word* going to lead me? It led me to Mary.

As I began to realize I was "Mary-bound," I examined the word itself while pilgrimaging toward her. Yes, compassion. It means to share a passion, to share a pain, to be part of the pain, part of the passion. As I finally came to Mary, I rested at her feet and looked at her and I realized suddenly what this word com-passion meant. It meant Mary.

Mary was born without the taint of original sin. This does not mean that she didn't have a free choice between good and evil throughout her life. She did have that free choice, otherwise her *fiat* would not have been freely given—would not have been the freewill offering that it was. I realized that her life with Jesus, which was freely embraced, was not easy. It was not easy because she did not always understand what many of the events of his life meant. What did his reply to her in the temple mean when he was a boy? What did he mean when he said to her one day that he had no brothers or sisters or mother? No, she didn't always understand, but she kept all his words in her heart, which meant that she loved him intensely and that he was her life.

Mary was the still one, the quiet one, the recollected one. She didn't speak much for she was also the listening one, and that is why she could keep so many of his words in her heart.

The still ones, the listening ones, are the children of the Father, and do his will. Mary was the mother of the Son, the daughter of the Father, and the spouse of the Holy Spirit. Yes, she was the listening, the praying, the still one above all others. She was also the free one, pure of heart, and therefore she saw God. Yes, Mary quite definitely must have seen God in many ways. Often darkly, as in a glass; perhaps occasionally in a blinding revelation of love.

But this is speculation. What isn't speculation is that she followed Christ in his passion.

When one considers Christ's passion (and I did in my poustinia on this occasion), one has to ask, what *is* passion? Passion holds hands with love. Passion makes love sparkle and shine, leading it to the rugged tops of immense mountains that lie in the hearts of men but can only be scaled by passionate lovers. Its roots are love, its fruit is love. Christ loved us passionately, and some of us love him back passionately.

Passion usually means pain. Nothing strange about that. Love and passion not only hold hands, not only scale the tops of rugged mountains, but they are entwined one around the other. There is no love without pain, and no pain without love. One without the other is inconceivable: love without pain is inconceivable.

Mary enters into this marriage of love and passion which the Lord accepted and through which he redeemed us. Pure of heart, she saw God. She followed him, her Son, right to the foot of the cross, and beyond to his grave. Hers was a com-passion. She shared his passion not only in a physical way but also in a spiritual, emotional, and deeply tragic way.

As I sat at Mary's feet and watched her with the eyes of my heart, I realized that a fantastic question had been presented to her. It took faith to accept that first announcement of the angel which told her that she was full of grace and that God would be born of her. Mary had that faith. Of her own free will she accepted to be the mother of the Messiah. Her faith was challenged too when, from the height of the cross, she heard Jesus say, "Woman, behold your son!" and to John, "Behold, your mother." Once more she was asked to do the impossible—or almost the impossible. The Son who had come to do the will of his Father was offering this same will of the Father to Mary.

At that moment he was telling her that she was to be the mother of mankind, and that her com-passion would be constantly exercised throughout the centuries, even as the mercy of God was going to be exercised throughout the ages. She too would have to forgive the present murderers of her Son and all the new murderers who would arise down through every generation. Our Lady's com-passion had to bear fruit, the fruit of forgiveness, and these two had to help heal mankind. Yes, the role of Mary was clarified for me a little more on this sunny poustinia day.

I remembered that many had asked me what compassion was. Now I felt that I was ready to tell them. It was Mary. Mary who experienced the passion of her Son as no one else experienced it. She truly com-passionated—she shared the passion of her Son. She shared his passionate love for humanity and for mankind, and she shared his pain!

"Passionate love for mankind" and "pain." These two realities were like a chalice the Father had given Christ from which men would drink and know that he had forgiven them. Forgiveness too is the fruit of love. The incredible, incomprehensible love of God is filled with forgiveness. This same chalice was also given to Mary. Somehow, in the incredible mystery of God's dealings with men, this woman was asked to share in the love, pain, forgiveness and the healing which her Son experienced on the cross.

Because Mary accepted this role, if role it be, she became the mother of men, and men understood that they could not walk through life without her. Men need other human beings, and they need above all a gentle one, a compassionate one, a listening one. They need a woman who could teach them forgiveness, because she forgave with all the fullness of her being. She forgave with the forgiveness of her Son. Yes, this would heal them, for nothing really heals like a woman can.

13

Touching Neighbor

God's Icebreakers

There is no denying it—the hunger for God is upon us! It always was with us, but now, throughout our apostolate —throughout the world—one can sense and feel its beautiful growth. Everywhere prayer has truly become "like an incense arising to God from every heart." It seems that all of us have "truly arisen," and begun in earnest toward that pilgrimage that we are called to undertake, and which forms part of our mandate. Let us, therefore, all thank God together! May his holy name be praised!

This is also the time when we have to open our minds, hearts and souls wide to the wind, the fire of the Holy Spirit. For there is no denying that he is truly abroad in all lands; and in some strange and mysterious fashion and in a very special way, among us in the apostolate of Madonna House. We have to prepare ourselves for a new journey to a higher mountain. Or perhaps, I should say, for a new dimension of loving and serving.

The vision that presents itself to me or "grows within me" these days is somewhat different and appears as a new dimension of love, as a pilgrimage to a higher plateau of the same mountain. You see, we are entering the "Ice

Age." It will not be very long before Canada and the U.S.A., and factually the world at large, will allow their governments—demand their governments!—to take over from cradle to grave all that we call the corporal works of mercy. This has already happened in several countries in Europe, and it is clearly discernible to eyes that see the horizon of our New World.

I call it the "Ice Age" because the corporal works of mercy should be done with great love, gentleness, understanding, compassion and delicacy. True, they rarely have been so performed, but in many instances they were. In the very near future, however, all the above nouns will be encompassed by one word: efficiency.

"Efficiency" is a very cold word, as is bureaucracy. True, no one will starve. No one will die for lack of medical care. Sweden, Denmark and Norway are good examples of this. Senior citizens, babies, little children and everyone in between are looked after competently, and there is no poverty, as we know it, in these countries. Soon, it shall be like this with us on this side of the Atlantic.

But there is coldness, terrible, icy coldness in all those places and in those countries. It is a coldness that begets a terrible loneliness in people, a loneliness and alienation which is followed by a high suicide rate. We must get ready by prayer and fasting, by a kenosis, by a self-emptying, to acquire pure and childlike hearts, hearts that are able to see God and thus able to enter this coming ice age. We must become harbingers and carriers of the fire of the Holy Spirit, for it is fire that melts ice. That will be our role in the future, and in not a too distant future at that.

We must prepare to be God's icebreakers. Each one of us must be prepared to become "God's Inn" for the millions of people who are already, even today, to be found lying wounded and lonely and beaten up by countless robbers whose name in truth is legion. Yes, we must become icebreakers whose hearts are so full of love of God and man, so filled with the fire of the Holy Spirit, that they can penetrate the terrible cold that already envelops us, and will imprison more and more the hearts of men.

In the years to come, a growing stream of people will come to us. They will not come for food or clothing or shelter. They will come because they have finally understood that man does not live by bread alone. Let us be very careful, then, of prejudging or discriminating against people. Yes, there might be dangers connected with the drug addict, violent people and so forth. But faith must carry us through—faith must carry us through—faith and love. Youth will come in search of listening hearts, in search of the wounds of Christ which alone can heal them. Our modern generation must touch before it will believe. We must have those wounds to show them so that they touch them and are touched and healed by Christ.

We must be ready, for this hospitality, this openness, will be the icebreakers and the inns that we must allow to grow in us through the Fire of Love. I see a multitude coming to us from all parts of the world, knocking at our doors. We must be ready, ready to let crowds pass through our hearts. Crowds with dirty feet, clean feet, broken feet, broken hearts, hungry souls.

Yes, men and women will come because they will want to touch, they will want to feel. As we journey toward the Absolute, we will become "God's icebreakers," and we will bring light, fire and warmth into the cold and ever more mechanical world of tomorrow where everyone is taken care of most competently and "efficiently." We are being chosen for a new dimension of love. We are being chosen to enter into that loneliness of modern man, that ice age of tomorrow, and become God's icebreakers and inns for all the wounded and frozen ones, so that they might be thawed out by our love.

Go, Speak with Tongues!

One Friday I was in the poustinia. I was praying for quite a while, conscious only of a void, an emptiness within. Slowly, very slowly, a thought formed. At first amorphous, then gently, like a spring breeze, it clarified itself, and I knew what the word of the Lord was for me: "Go, speak with tongues!"

Strange as this may seem, I didn't accept those words immediately, but spent quite some time meditating on them. To me they were very important, because as a Russian I had always felt more inclined to pray for the gift of tears than the gift of tongues. But the words and the sentence persisted, and so did my meditation. What follows is how I saw the Lord's words for me.

A long time ago, in ages long passed, men in their pride and arrogance had brought together brick and mortar to build a tower that would reach heaven. This was their way, evidently, of showing the Lord that they could reach heaven by their own efforts, by their own production.

But the Lord came and looked at these men in their tower and was greatly displeased. He showed his displeasure by giving the people a "gift of tongues." It wasn't a gift but a punishment. Instead of uniting them, it disunited them, for suddenly, each spoke a different language. Because they couldn't understand one another, the tower remained uncompleted; in time it fell into ruins. It was a monument to pride, to the folly of arrogance, a warning that man should not evaluate himself by his productivity

alone. I imagine too that a greater tragedy must have be-
fallen them: they could not praise God because of their
disunity.

Time passed, and a prophet came and predicted a new
age and a day of Yahweh. Joel was his name. He said
that he had a message for the people from the Lord: "You
will know that I am in the midst of Israel, that I am Yahweh
your God, with none equal to me. My people will not be
disappointed anymore. I will pour out my Spirit on all
mankind. Your sons and daughters shall prophesy, your
old men shall dream dreams and your young men shall see
visions. Even on the slaves, men and women, I will pour
out my Spirit in those days. I will display portents in
heaven and on earth" (3:1-3).

Again, time marched on. The day of Pentecost which
Jesus predicted to his apostles came to pass. "When Pentecost came around, they had all met in one room, when
suddenly they heard what sounded like a powerful wind
from heaven, the noise of which filled the whole house in
which they were sitting; and something appeared to them
that seemed like tongues of fire; these separated and came
to rest on the head of each of them. They were all filled
with the Holy Spirit, and began to speak foreign languages
as the Spirit gave them the gift of speech (tongues)" (Acts
2:1-4).

God seemed to have a lot to do in the Old and New
Testaments with speech, languages. There is something
about speech and language that is evidently intensely important and very holy.

It isn't too important for us whether we accept literally
or not the story of the tower of Babel. It was what they
were talking about that was important. The Tower of
Babel is a symbol of division, of splitting, of turning away

from God. It was the breaking of the commandment of love of God and love of neighbor.

It seemed to me as I sat in my poustinia that throughout the history of man's growth there was some sort of unity. All men, down through the ages, have believed in Someone greater than themselves. All men praised God. The various shapes and forms their belief and praises took need not concern us. The great fact was: man believed, man prayed.

Somewhere along the path of humanity's growth a serpent entered once again and enticed again with the appealing apple: "You are equal to God." Some ate that apple again and became proud and arrogant. They decided to show God that they could reach him by a man-made tower that would reach to the heavens.

Things hadn't changed too much! Same invitation, same answer. Only this time man lost the language of love that speaks to all peoples in every tongue, in every language across the world. I sat in my poustinia and watched love speaking all languages, and then saw it vanish because so many didn't wish to love, didn't wish to accept love. I finally got very tired of thinking of this tower of Babel as the symbol of man's division, of his breaking faith, or this splintering of the worship and praise of God, of this fragmentation of love for his fellowman. Yes, I grew very, very tired.

But I went on praying, because deep down somewhere, beyond the range of my understanding, beyond the range of my knowledge, I knew without knowing, I understood without understanding, that *Pentecost was God's gift of healing*. He had given us an Advocate, but also a healer, for he sent forth his Spirit to make all things new again. And my heart rejoiced!

Yes, I have to go and speak with the *tongues of love* to everybody. It is through loving my neighbor that the gift of tongues will become incarnated, will take flesh as a skeleton does. It is not only that men and women will speak in tongues unknown to one another at prayer meetings, and that this unknown language will praise God. I have nothing against that. But in my poustinia I felt so deeply, with some sort of anguish and yet joy, that, in truth, we have to speak with tongues of love. We have to because we believe. We have faith. It is because we believe that we speak, as St. Paul said, "I believed and therefore I spoke."

We must speak because we must love. Our speech is a gift of God to all through each one of us. Remember, he said: "Open your mouth and I will fill it." More charisms are being given to people, and the more such charisms are multiplied, the more will men render thanksgiving and glory to God and praise him.

Yes, I saw very clearly that we have to enter into a dimension of faith that perhaps is new to us. A dimension that would make us walk the yet untrodden path of translating the gift of the Holy Spirit, the gift of tongues, into the gift of love—our love for every person we meet. So, *speaking with tongues* became for me on this Friday in my poustinia a *gift of love*. I understood that before I can offer that gift to my brother, I have to open my two hands and put them together like a cup and lift them up to receive that gift from the Holy Trinity.

To each one of us, at all times, the gift of tongues is given. We must never forget that it is also a gift of love. What was seemingly destroyed by God on that day when men built for themselves the tower of Babel, is being restored to men to build themselves a tower of love, a stairway of love, not only to reach heaven but to pierce it and return to earth. The kingdom of God which is the kingdom of love begins here and now.

Strange, that at this point I understood that the gift of tongues or the gift of speech is given to those who are silent, still, and listening to God. Strange that silence and stillness should be the cradle of speech. But that is how it seemed to me!

Then I looked deeper. The word "cradle" aroused much attention, my inner attention, and I came to Mary, the Mother of God. Pentecost is also Mary's feast, for the Holy Spirit truly overshadowed her. It is through him that Jesus entered her womb. She was the spouse of the Holy Spirit. As I meditated on Mary I realized why the words "listening, silence, waiting" dropped into my heart as drops of a strange perfume. For now I was led to Mary who was the silent one, the listening one, the loving one, the waiting one. I understood too, though dimly, that it was not a cradle of my heart or yours that I was talking about or thinking about. It was the cradle of her womb from which he who was a gift to all men, whatever tongue they spoke, had come forth.

I realized at that moment that the gift of tongues was really Jesus Christ himself, for he is love, and once I speak of the gift of tongues I speak of love, of Jesus, of his Father, and of the Holy Spirit. In a word, I speak of the Trinity. But Jesus Christ is the Gift because God the Father gave him to us out of love for us, and God the Son keeps revealing, clarifying his Father to us. What was proud and arrogant in us who continually try to build towers of Babel with the help of the ever-present serpent had been healed by love, by God, by Jesus Christ.

Yes, I saw it and I understood it. Just thinking of it makes me praise the Trinity, especially the Father for so loving us as to send his Son who was love, so that we might understand that the gift of tongues is the gift of love. It doesn't mean only, I repeat, speaking in strange sounds. No. It means loving one another, for love transcends all speech. Love shines in a clasp of two hands. If men become icons of Christ, love shines. If we pray to the Holy Spirit, and then forget we are praying because we have become immersed in him, "we become a prayer." The gift of tongues is now interiorized. Anyone who comes near us understands this type of speech. Not that we matter very much, but God does in us, and the men around us listen to the gift of tongues. They hear the speech of God with man directly or through other men.

Yes, the gift of tongues is the gift beyond all measuring because it is the gift of God himself. Strangely enough, the gift of tongues must translate itself into speech. As St. Paul says, in the passage already quoted, "I believed and therefore I spoke." His way of speaking, even as the way of the other apostles who had received the gift of tongues on Pentecost, was clear to those who heard them. It was clear because they loved or truly had begun to love. Love does such things—love and faith.

Let us not be afraid to speak in our own language or in body language. God will make it understandable to all. Because when we begin to speak in tongues for the glory of God, a mystery beyond all knowing takes place in us. *We* cease to speak and *God* speaks. That is why everyone will rejoice because that kind of gift of tongues will shake men, as shake them it should. For it means that another human being—a brother, a sister—has handed himself over to God totally, has believed that his own language—English, French, Ukrainian, or what have you—can convey God's words to the heart of another. They who speak it have believed in the Lord. They have opened their mouths and have allowed him to speak even though his words were like fire in their hearts, fire that seemed to scorch everything it touches. And yet, after they have stopped talking, they knew that fire to be the fire of the Holy Spirit who filled them to overflowing.

The apostles had fire descend upon their heads. We today, who want to speak in tongues, must allow that fire to go through us and cleanse us and come forth from our mouths. Yes, that is what we must do.

As all this opened before me in my meditation, I felt such a joy I could not contain it. I understood that he was sending forth his Spirit even through me, and you, and everybody else. We know, as long as we cooperate with the Spirit, that we will truly renew the face of the earth. It is then that I also understood the theme of my day in the poustinia. The thought the Lord was giving me when he said, "Go, speak with tongues." Alleluia!

Selfish Silences

I want to explain to you, though you might already know that no two poustinias are alike. Some are full of joy, light, and peace; others, on the contrary, are full of heaviness, inability to think, even with one's head in one's heart, as I always say one should think. My last poustinia was different again. The word came slowly. It was a heavy word that fell on my heart like a piece of lead. The word was "silence."

But it was not the silence that I have often written about before—the silence of love, the silence of lovers with one another, the silence of man's heart speaking to God, as it were, by silences. No, it was not that kind of silence. Perhaps it was the other "face" of silence, for I think that silence has many faces. Anyhow, this kind of silence had another face. It was simply there.

First and foremost, the face of this silence revealed itself as an *escape*. You know that when people are trying to escape from something that seems dangerous to them, they walk very silently. No one speaks, not even in whispers. Usually they choose a time when people cannot watch them or see them. They like the night. Not necessarily the physical night. I am speaking symbolically. They like the darkness of their own night to escape from contact with others, to escape from carrying the pain of others. Everything about this "silence of escape" is, therefore, underhanded, subtle, guarded.

I meditated on all this. What was the Lord trying to tell me in my poustinia? I couldn't figure it out. So my thoughts turned to a book called *A Terrible Beauty* by James Carroll. In it this good priest says that conversion means "turning roundabout." It means to stop running away. It means changing one's course and going *toward* Someone instead of running *away* from someone.

As I meditated on his words, the silence of escape became clearer. What kind of escape was this that so many of us were engaged in so quietly, so silently? It became clear to me that it was an escape from facing the other. We still do not want to break this silence open. We still do not want to open the doors or curtains which we constantly keep closed between us.

The silence of escape which I was facing in my poustinia was a silence in which one door after another was quietly closing behind us. The door was well oiled ahead of time so that there was no sound. Soundlessly we close those doors, one after another, thus escaping from sharing ourselves, from ceasing to be individuals and becoming a community in which closed doors cannot exist. Of course, I am speaking of closing doors in a spiritual sense. We have not yet become completely converted to love so that we can engage in communication with the other in a loving silence that is quite open, wide open.

I pondered this strange new face of silence that began to reveal itself to me. The more I pondered the sadder I became. In fact, I became even sorrowful because I realized that this face was also true, and that we are still trying to escape from one another in this stealthy silence of ours. Oh, we have progressed I know. from years past. Progressed a hundred, perhaps a thousand percent. Yet I saw clearly in my poustinia that there is still among us a strange attraction to periodically escape confrontation with one another. We are not ready, it seems to me, to let our silence speak as lovers speak to each other, as members of a community should, precisely because they are lovers of God and of one another. Yes, I saw this continual stealth of our silence that wants to run away from others and also from God—if not completely, at least in part.

I prayed. What else was there to do? But again this silence dared to show me still another aspect of its face. It was the aspect of hostility, of anger, and I understood that one can be silent while anger, hostility, rejection are filling and searing our souls. I realized that that type of silence, in fact, is a thousand times worse than speech—open, angry, resentful speech. It is a sort of deadly silence that separates instead of unites, that can deal a deathblow to love without a single syllable being uttered. I shivered and became cold in the face of that silence; yet I praised the Lord, for I didn't really believe it was among us. Then I prayed that it would never be.

Even as I was praying I saw yet another aspect of this strange silence: the silence of indifference. It's a kind of silence that seemed to say without words that one didn't care too much about things or people. It's a sort of mutism that didn't say yes, didn't say no. It was an apathetic silence which said in its own silent way that it was too much trouble to be anything or to really do anything for God or for others.

Such silence manifested a certain tiredness, but a sort of mental, neurotic tiredness which serves to add to the silence among us.

Just when I thought that I had seen quite a few of the aspects of this heavy silence, still another dimension appeared: the silence of fear! It was the fear that makes one turn to the silence of escape, of stealth, of compromise, of rationalization! This is not the kind of fear that is the beginning of wisdom. Oh no! The fear *of the Lord* is the beginning of wisdom. This kind of fear is compassionate, gentle, is concerned about the pain and vulnerability of others, is interested in the difficulties and problems of others. This is what is meant by "the fear of the Lord is the beginning of wisdom." If you love someone you will be afraid to hurt that person, and this fear is not servile.

No, we are not speaking of this kind of fear. The fear that came to me was a slavish fear, a fear that made one turn to silence as an escape, the silence of stealth, of compromise, of rationalization. When I met this silence I was almost afraid of it, because it meant or pointed to a fear of God that was unhealthy. It was forgetful that God was all-merciful, all-forgiving. It was a fear that held us tight, and in this silence of fear the love and mercy of God was removed. This silence of fear was the silence of faithlessness—the silence due to lack of faith.

Suddenly that whole other side of silence became clear to me in the poustinia, and I realized that silence could be evil and could proceed from the Evil One. I perceived that it might have begun as an escape, but it would end in becoming a turmoil of doubt, misery and lack of faith. And, of course, it would also cease to be silent and become an inner noise that could not be stilled.

I didn't want to write this word to you, but then I would have passed by in silence myself something that should be shared between us. For there should be no closed doors, no curtains put up. We must be opened all the way, even unto our deep pains.

Trust

The passage I was reading in the poustinia on this occasion was from Paul's Second Letter to the Corinthians:

> Thin sowing means thin reaping. The more you sow, the more you reap. Each one should give what he has decided in his own mind, not grudgingly or because he is made to, for God loves a cheerful giver, and there is no limit to the blessings which God can send you. He will make sure you will always have all you need for yourself in every possible circumstance, and still have something to spare for all sorts of good works. As scripture says, "He was free in almsgiving and gave to the poor; his good deeds will never be forgotten.' The one who provides seed for the sower and bread for food will provide you with all the seed you want and make the harvest of your good deeds a larger one and made richer in every way. You will be able to do all the generous things which, through us, are the cause of thanksgiving to God (9:6-12)

About four o'clock in the afternoon the word came to me: trust.

I have read this letter of St. Paul many times. But this time I began to think seriously of seeds, of planting, of reaping, of wheat, of flour, of bread, of grapes, of wine, of almsgiving, and there was a sort of rhythmic pattern of thoughts in my mind. They followed one another without difficulty.

Then suddenly I stopped. I noticed something I hadn't seen before. There were other things besides bread, wine, seed and food to give our brothers. Yes, such things were necessary in times of poverty, famine and difficulties. But another sentence popped into my head: "Not by bread alone does man live."

I looked at the world today, at all of us, at all the people I have ever seen in my travels, at all those who came to Madonna House, and I realized that indeed this last sentence was truth itself. In America and Canada and in other countries, the hungry and the naked are being taken care of by insurance, welfare and social security. Yet, men are hungry for something seemingly more vital and necessary than bread!

Human loneliness descended upon me in my poustinia. I couldn't tell you if it was a moment or an hour, but I understood what created this loneliness and made it like a hunger in the heart of man, like a sore in his body: *Man felt that he was unimportant*. He walked amongst other men and noticed that no one paid attention to him. Oh, they passed the time of day and they said a few words like, "How are you?" "Okay." "I'm okay and you're okay. Everything is okay." And they go on their way. Sometimes they speak about the weather. Sometimes they talk of their problems. But there doesn't seem to be any in-depth interest in the other. Men walk around as if they are invisible to each other.

John Donne has said that no man is an island. In our large cities, however, and even in our countrysides, millions upon millions of little islands are walking and floating around, touching each other for a second, only to separate again, to continue walking and floating around by themselves.

I tried to understand. Suddenly I discovered the things that were more important than bread, things that we can give to one another: faith in God, trust in one another, love, hope. This is the true almsgiving that men must give to each other today.

I suddenly felt that I could walk from island to island and give this faith, love, hope and trust to the other. How could I do it? It wasn't going to be easy—that was clear from the beginning. My fellowmen are not used to receiving such gifts. They don't realize the wealth of such gifts, nor that they have to give them themselves to everyone—poor, young, rich, everyone in the world. These are the gifts men truly hunger for, but not everyone realizes it.

Yet, most of us know how important it is to feel that someone believes in us and loves us. We know what it is to want to be loved personally, and honestly. We don't want to be loved simply as part of some nebulous humanity, and that because Christ said so. We want to be loved as if there were no one else but us.

Yes, I must give not only money, not only bread, not only clothing, not only good deeds, but I have to give myself. The only way I can do it is by giving my love, my trust, my hope to man, by having faith in him as God has faith in him.

How does one go about giving trust? Well, it is very

simple, really, when you come right down to it. Trust is the fruit of love. But it is the easiest, the simplest fruit which every man can touch if you give it to him. They can feel it, as man feels bread and wine or gold when these are being offered. Even though this gift is transcendent and spiritual, it is somehow able to be felt, because it comes forth in day-to-day relationships of one to the other. That is to say, relationships with our neighbors, with our brothers and sisters. So . . . trust! To open our hearts to trust the untrustworthy, to accept people as they are, to find myself shortchanged and in spite of this to trust again —all this is not easy. But that is what we have to do!

Trust again and again and again, as God trusts us. If man gives his trust to another, and people give their trust to people, then the very act of trusting can make another person a bit more trustworthy than they were before. As the trust continues—joyous, smiling, simple, ordinary trust— the one to whom it is given begins to straighten up and look at himself and find in himself something that he never thought of finding before—that he is trustworthy in spite of his failings! He realizes this because someone trusts him!

Yes, the word is trust, and it applies to us, because trust is the sun that should arise with us every morning and go to sleep with us every night. Trust will open our hearts as the real sun opens flowers in a garden. Each of us is a beautiful flower in God's garden. Alas, so many of us hold on tight to being a bud. We are buds that don't want to unfold because we are afraid of what happens to a flower when it unfolds and opens up. We are afraid of bees or other insects that may come and take our nectar away. We seem to want to keep all of it for ourselves; if we do we will die. But we cannot open up unless we trust somebody. Let me paraphrase somewhat one of the lines from St.

Paul: "Each one should give what he has decided in his own mind. Is it trust? Is it love? Is it hope? All these lead to faith."

If we trust somebody we are truly opening the way to love, hope and faith. For God loves a cheerful giver, and there is no limit to the blessing God can give us. He will always make sure that we have what we need for ourselves. That is to say, that when we give cheerfully, joyfully, of ourselves, of our faith, of our love, then indeed we become truly alive. We become so full that we are like a granary. Others can come and take the grain away. For us especially in Madonna House, who are exposed to so many people who come, we must give out of the treasury that God has given us. We must pass on his trust in us to them, his love for us to them, the gift of hope we have to them.

But the word "trust" is an immense word. For if men begin to trust one another, then they will stop killing one another with mental cruelty and every kind of inhumanity. Thus did the word "trust" stand before me, smiling, asking to be given away, because obviously I could never give it away. Whenever you give it away, God replenishes it anew. Like love, trust can only be kept by being given away.

So let us all go into the depth of ourselves and find out if we trust one another, and if not, why not. Let us talk about it, shall we? For charity begins at home you know, and the almsgiving of trust starts with us.

Poustinia in a Hospital

God always opens new doors. I never realized that a hospital room could be a poustinia. But it is, even physically. The bed, the table, the chair—these are the simple furnishings of hospital rooms, very much like the furnishings of the poustinia. In the hospital there may or may not be a bible. It is usually available on request, but perhaps the person in the hospital room cannot read, for a thousand reasons. But reading is not important in such a poustinia. I mean reading with your eyes. Because in a hospital room, in the poustinia of pain and death, Christ becomes himself the Word, the Book, and nothing else, *nothing else* is necessary.

One is confined to one room. Although various nurses and doctors come into that poustinia, they are really like shadows flitting back and forth. One person remains— Christ. The rest are, I repeat, shadows, etched on a wall. A nurse with a thermometer; another with some medicines; doctors probing and talking; once in a while you are placed in a wheelchair and wheeled to an X-ray department or to some other place. All this does not interfere with the understanding, the deep sense, the realization, that one is now really face to face with God, and in a true poustinia, not only a physical poustinia but the desert of one's own life. This is the moment of realization in regard to the interiorization that one has to make of the gospel, placing his very life in and on it. These are the moments when, reading the words of Jesus Christ himself, one also reads in him one's life.

There are strange moments in this strange poustinia— where suddenly the physical pains, all kinds of pains, not only one's own but those of the people located right next to you, seem to become yours . . they become mine. The reading of my life in these surroundings close to God's heart became vivid and clear.

Now I became, in a manner of speaking, my own physician. Or did I? Is it perhaps that Christ the healer, the physician, comes at such a time and teaches you lessons and gives you remedies far beyond any that the medical profession can give you?

For let us be clear: in the poustinia of a hospital room you and I are truly faced with the question of life and death!

In Ward 1, someone is faced with blindness. The despair of the one who just heard this verdict entered my soul. It didn't make any difference whether the patient was young or old. Neither age nor sex mattered. *Only the fact of blindness brought me as it might have brought them to the edge of despair.*

Then there is the one who just heard that he has cancer. Suddenly into my own poustinia his pain entered, and I began to understand vividly what it is, or what it might be, to have a terminal or crippling disease. Now I began to pray over the new aspects of pain which hadn't entered my own life but which I dimly shared with others (I had been a nurse and had helped in many ways just such people that surrounded me now).

But oh, the vividness, the tremendous blinding flash of understanding that came to me in that poustinia in my hospital room!

Now, by the grace of God, I understood clearly what blindness and semiblindness was, not only physical but spiritual.

I reread the parable of the blind man and it became a reality to me. It was I who couldn't read. It was I who had this curtain over my eyes. It was I who was filled with the misery of the blind man in the gospel.

Just at the moment when this misery shook me, when I almost cried out because I couldn't even vicariously carry this cross which alas has fallen on so many of my brothers and sisters in the world, light penetrated my blindness. Relief came from their pains and the need to be the bearer of other people's pain became so self-evident that I wondered why I ever doubted it.

But somehow I was attracted, directed, especially to the pain of blindness, and I understood that a blind man could be a lamp to my neighbor's feet and illumine the darkness of another. Now alone in that hospital poustinia I began to understand that spiritual darkness, the rejection of God, and all the things that we are so apt to discuss today are illogical: even while I seem to reject God or you . . . seem to have lost faith in him or you . . . I still can be a light to another man's feet.

I remembered at that moment part of the story from *Crime and Punishment* written by Dostoevsky, when the murderer came to visit a prostitute. He was amazed that she had an icon with a vigil light burning in front of it. He asked her if she believed in God, and she, while disrobing, was incensed by his question. She answered, definitely, and with deep faith, "How could I live if I didn't believe in God?"

At this moment I knew that I was right and this knowledge was given to me by God: *a blind man can be a light to his neighbor's feet.*

Yes, in the poustinia of the hospital you drift off to sleep and back again and during that sleep God gives you understanding. The man filled with cancer, whom you dimly remember, suddenly becomes one with you. You feel sort of united with him, and again you cry out in agony, voicing as it were, his own agony, but realizing that because you did, he ceased to be alone—and so did you.

It is as if the part of his body that is filled with cancer becomes your body. It is you now instead of him who faces in the night of the subdued lights of a hospital room death for cancer may be terminal and death is always before you

All this tragedy that is going on three doors down becomes yours, suddenly, in your poustinia of the hospital. And you read with clarity in the heart of God the pain of others, for as with everything else, all the pain of the world is reflected in God.

But strangely enough, as you lie awake in your hospital poustinia in the night, and begin to understand death by coming closer to it in others, you also see that physical cancer is nothing compared to the terrible cancer that grows in the hearts of so many of us all over the world.

It happened to me, and before my mind's eye I saw the terrible cancer that grows over politics, economics, our whole strange, tragic life on earth, that always seems to end in wars and slaughter and violence. Yes, that cancer became vivid and clear in my hospital poustinia.

But above all, in this hospital room which I had transformed from within into a poustinia, I faced death, for it is quite obvious that in hospitals you face death. Inevitably so. Maybe your own. Maybe someone else's. It makes no difference.

For what reason did my hospital room suddenly turn into a poustinia? It was obvious. To face pain and death. I understood then that death isn't an intruder, but a wonderful novice master. It isn't life which is a phenomenon of death, but it is death which is a provisionary phenomenon of life.

The saints faced death with joy because they understood they were born into the kingdom of God. In the hospital room which I made into a poustinia, death became real and friendly; a bridge between the now and forever! Death became the freedom from all those ills I was surrounded by, but it became more! It became life and joy. God has reserved the secret of the hereafter, for it is said that neither ear has heard nor eyes have seen the joy God has reserved for those who love him.

But above all, death sings of the mercy of God. I asked myself if just for a moment I thought that the mercy of God ended at the moment of my death and I laughed aloud at two a.m. in a hospital room that became a poustinia because I realized this couldn't happen. How could it! It's just impossible, for the mercy of God extends to heaven, to purgatory and hell.

I was reading a book by Evdokimov. and I was struck by his beautiful description of what purgatory is. He says, "It is a place of maturation." In a manner of speaking, it is like my hospital room, but much more poor and simple where the Great Physician opens the eyes of your soul to the joy of himself.

It is a place where you begin to really understand that there is no time, for it is a place without time and there is no time in the hereafter. To God a million years are like a day. He takes time and throws it out for those who have passed the Great Divide. In purgatory, therefore, there is maturation, and obviously no fire and no pain as we have been led to believe. In order to make people mature you use love, gentleness and tenderness. Therefore. I realized that purgatory is simply a slow growth, and God has it take place even while we are on earth.

The Body of Christ is the Church Triumphant Militant and Suffering, if you want to call maturation suffering. It begins here and continues in the hereafter.

Yet lying in my hospital poustinia room I understood more. I understood hell is not excluded from the all-merciful eyes of God, and I remembered that Judas brought light into hell for he received the body and blood of Christ at the Last Supper and it was still with him there, lighting hell. It seemed impossible to me that God will not forgive the devil at the last judgment. The great saints, especially of the East and the Fathers of the Church and the Desert, prayed for that forgiveness. Why shouldn't we?

In the poustinia many, many things became clear.

While I was there I composed a little poem called "Poustinia in the Hospital" on October 21, 1973:

> A room, a bed, two chairs
> Stark, naked room of pain
> A room set all apart
> For just that pain,
> In a desert more real
> Than the deserts of sand and heat.
> Poustinias indeed where man meets his God
> Face to face
> Both crucified.
> Gone are all subterfuges, excuses, rationalizations.
> Now man enters into the truth of God.
> All his masks are torn and man becomes what
>   he truly is.
> Poustinias in a hospital of Golgotha
> On which the crucified God is planted in the midst
> of crucified men.
> Now is the moment of meeting,
> Now is the moment of speaking.
> But no words are needed in the poustinia of
>   a hospital room.
> Only the steps of the Father
> And the light
> Of the Spirit
> That comes
> Like a gentle breeze
> In the spring,

Consoling,
Assuaging,
Making clear
All that was unclear
So that
In a stark,
Naked
Room of pain
Joy enters.
The sick arise
And dance with Christ.

Part IV

The Heart of the
Poustinia

14

My Own Poustinik Vocation

In the early part of March, 1973, I wrote a very special letter—word from the poustinia—to my community of Madonna House. For the purposes of this book I could easily have adapted the contents to the reader. However, since my vocation is integrally bound up with the Madonna House Community, I have decided to keep the letter in that context. With a little imagination, I'm sure you will find it easy to apply it to yourself, you who also have been driven, by your restlessness, to set out on your pilgrimage toward God.

"Dear Family,

"This letter from the poustinia is a very special one. I hope you read it together slowly and in a sense with an open heart, and reverently, because it is one of those letters that perhaps is written once in a lifetime under the guidance of the Holy Spirit. It deeply concerns you and me and the plan that the Lord has for us. I hope it explains a little further what the poustinia is, and shows how slowly God brought you into the poustinia through me, and how your understanding of this letter will indeed make God's harvest richer and help to restore his Church.

"This is March 2, 1973, but I'm not positive. In the poustinia time goes very quickly, and an hour is a lifetime and a lifetime is an hour. I have to face a few things today that are not easy to face. They are not easy to explain because there are some things about them that are strange.

"Last night I went (because the manager personally invited me) to see the movie *Nicholas and Alexandra*. It is a take-off from the book on the tsar and the tsarina. I can't say that I was too excited about it. It's difficult for me to see all those Russian things. I didn't stay until the end.

"I was surprised on the way back from Barry's Bay to Madonna House. Such a feeling of total loneliness took hold of me that I was really astonished. I am lonely. I have been lonely many, many times. But this time it was a sort of strange loneliness, a loneliness that held me like a vise and shook me.

"I looked at the road. It was like any other Russian road. The trees were like the trees at home. The hills were very similar to what I remembered I had left. I don't know about other people's experience, but suddenly I realized with a most extraordinary realization that I was a stranger in a strange country. There was no denying it, no way of softening the impression, making it easier to bear. In the midst of nowhere, or shall we say, in the midst of a beautiful Canadian countryside, I was torn apart with an extraordinary longing for the Russia I had left over 50 years ago. And the further amazing thing was that now, somehow, it didn't matter anymore!

"When we returned home all I wanted to do was to get to my poustinia. I collected my things, went in, and closed the door.

"Now I began to realize something that I hadn't known before: the poustinia, the desert (for that is what it is) brings back memories, memories of a thousand things which we think we have completely forgotten.

"Memories of Russia. The smell of the earth in the fall; the walks through the forest on carpets of leaves made of a thousand colors; the outskirts of villages; the sounds of village life floating through the brisk autumn air; the strident voices of old women, the teasing, laughing voices of the young; the sight of the church at the end of the village; the village itself, built in two rows, with each row of houses facing the other, with a sort of main street in the middle. And there, at the end of town, the village green where everybody met most of the evenings, and always on Sundays and holidays. Suddenly, there was the procession of Holy Saturday after the 12 gospels had been read, and there were the people coming back with their shaded tapers to light the one vigil light before the icon of Our Lady in their bedroom or main room. Funny, how all these memories were coming back tonight.

"But the realization that was overwhelming me most of all—like a sea in which I was drowning, now surfacing, now overcome by it again, now surfacing—the overwhelming wave or remembrance tonight was that *I was a stranger in a strange land*. There was no denying it. I lived with values different from other people. I was beginning to understand more deeply the darkness of which St. John of the Cross and St. Teresa of Avila speak. In such a darkness there is only one light, and that light is God. Unless you hold on to him, you become enmeshed in the meshes of the devil. For the first time since I have started coming to my poustinia, I knew that I was being tempted by self-pity. I also knew that the temptation was well directed because ever since I came to Canada I have been lonely, lonely with a cosmic loneliness of a refugee whom nobody understands or wishes to, and who perhaps was only understood after a long and arduous fight.

"Yes, I knew I was being tempted in the area where it hurts the most. The night became darker. The loneliness consumed me as it had for so many years. I did not know exactly what to do or where to turn. Across the river the community slept now. They had enjoyed, I'm sure, the garbled-up story of Nicholas and Alexandra, of the Cossacks and the Kronstadt and all the rest of it. How history can be distorted. It made you feel kind of sad. My loneliness increased.

"I fell asleep after a rough night, and the day was a little better. But I cannot say that this is exactly a peaceful poustinia. I think I have the key to my loneliness and I can see the lock, but I'm not sure if I can connect them yet. The key is very simple. I am a stranger in this land, in this world, by the gift of God. He has called me from my youth as he called Jesus his Son to go to Egypt. Christ was also a refugee, and so were his mother and foster-father. His foster-father was told to go because of the slaughter of the Innocents. I was told to go for a similar reason. I don't know who told us, but we just knew that we had to go. We *had* to go. There was nothing else left to do.

"The whole panorama of my journey unfolded itself before my eyes. I was young, 19 or so. Because of the slaughter of the innocents I was taken out of Russia by him. After many moons, as the Indians say, I was brought to this new land. In this new land and in all the lands before and after—in the States and in all my travels—I was a pilgrim. I was a solitary. *I was a poustinik, and I never knew it.*

"Perhaps that is where this strange vocation came from. Ever since I left Russia I have been a poustinik, a pilgrim. I have been fasting from the food of my language and of my people. I have been mortifying myself by adapting myself to the ways and manners of other people. And always I walked in solitude. *That was my true vocation—and I never understood it!* I did not understand that it was the vocation of loneliness, that God had invited me to share his loneliness because this was to be the vocation of many. Many people don't realize that their loneliness is an invitation to share the loneliness of God.

"I sat in my poustinia, dumbfounded, and wondered why I had not seen the whole pattern of my vocation. There were moments when I had dimly glimpsed it, as when I had sold all my possessions. I had glimpsed it during the moments when the Little Mandate* was being given to me throughout the years. I had glimpsed it when I thought of living alone and simply serving my brethren as the poustinikki now do here at Madonna House. When two men and three women came to join me in my apostolate those many

---

*The Little Mandate (below) is a series of "words" that came to me over the years. They are a sort of gospel summary, incarnating for the community of Madonna House the main features of our spirituality.

Arise—go! Sell all you possess. Give it directly, personally to the poor. Take up my cross (their cross) and follow me . . . going to the poor . . . being poor . . . being one with them . . . one with me.

Little—be always little! Be simple . . . poor . . . childlike.

Preach the gospel *with your life,* without compromise! Listen to the Spirit, he will lead you.

Do little things exceedingly well for love of me. Love . . love . . . love . . . never counting the cost. Go into the marketplace and stay with me. Pray, fast . . . pray always . . fast.

Be hidden. Be a light to your neighbor's feet. Go without fears into the depth of men's hearts. I shall be with you.

Pray always. I will be your rest.

years ago in Toronto, I thought that I had had the wrong idea about my vocation. Now I realized that *God gave me the vocation of a poustinik from the moment he took me out of Russia and brought me into a strange land.*

"Yes, that's it. That is why my heart hungered so much for the vocation of the poustinia, of the desert, of solitude, of prayer, of being a person of the towel and the water. No one understood what I desired with such a great desire except God. Funny, isn't it, that I had this vocation all the time I was seeking it! Only God can play such a strange joke on people. But it's a beautiful joke. Yes, I see it now. God invited me to share the Garden of Olives. He invited me to be in the High Priest's house. He invited me to stand at his side during Pontius Pilate's interrogation.

"A vision of Friendship House in Harlem and Friendship House in Toronto came before my eyes, but especially of the house in Harlem. There I used to lie on the floor at night and cry myself to sleep. What was the use of lying down in a bed with springs that jabbed you painfully, and when all the sadness and pain in the world was pouring into your soul? Better to lie on the floor and cry, cry until there were no tears left. Only now do I realize why I cried on that funny floor in Harlem. I cried because I had been taught long ago and far away that tears wash away the sin of the world. It just never occurred to me at the time that that was what I was doing. It never occurred to me that God had given me the *gift of tears.* No doubt, I cried for myself too, and for those who were persecuting me; that's the Russian way. But I didn't realize it.

"And then came Combermere. All through the years I was telling the Glad News to everyone who wanted to listen. Not many did at first, but still I continued to speak. Persecution, loneliness, pain, rejection——all the things that God had invited me to share with him before—were present again. The vocation that I had thought was mine, *really was mine*. I hadn't made a mistake, indeed I hadn't. On the contrary, I was right. Only I hadn't seen deeply enough into what was going on. In a sense, *the Lord had hidden it from me, as he always does*.

"But I was right. When I left Russia, I had already entered the poustinia. The poustinia that I sought, consciously or unconsciously, was somewhere deep down in the marrow of my bones. The Lord led me into the *poustinia of daily life*. And that is how today, at the beginning of March, 1973, I have suddenly seen this great light in the darkness of the night. My loneliness had a reason for its existence. It formed a poustinia not built by human hands but built by God himself. It is astonishing, simply astonishing, that I didn't see this at the time—I just didn't see it! How stupid can you get!

"Truly, through all these years, I have lived in a poustinia, in silence, in solitude. And what is even more astonishing, while I was living in it I was pilgrimaging in search of him, always in search of him, my Desired One. While I was searching, he was present, bringing me to Gethsemane, to the High Priest, to Pilate. Eventually I followed him, by both grace and desire, to Golgotha, where he presented me with three nails. I knew I had to accept them.

"Yes, today I have clarified something very important to myself—the essence of my vocation. Now I was wide awake. I said to myself:

"Yes, things have fallen into place. You realized today that the Lord really had given you the vocation that you thought he had given you when you went into the slums of Toronto. Already at that time he had made you a pilgrim.

He had taken you out of your land. He had brought you to a new land, a land that you came eventually to love—had loved, in fact, from the beginning—even though it was not your land. Yes, the Lord did that. He did it quietly and unobtrusively. There were so many refugees, and to all of them the same fate was allotted with slightly different accents. But yours was kind of special.

"And so you entered a strange land, and you were given silence. You were also given solitude. You were given the type of solitude which is spent in the midst of people. Like so many other Eastern notions, this also seems a bit incomprehensible to the Western world in which you now live—*but it will eventually be understood because God wants it to be understood.*

"Yes, he wants it to be understood. Solitude in the midst of the people is the Jesus Prayer, the prayer of the presence of God. It is the holding on to God in what may sometimes be a land of total despair, a real poustinia, a real desert, like the desert waste around Mount Sinai. Yes, he gave you all these things, and then he made you a pilgrim. This is what you wanted. This is what you thought you were going to get, because you knew it must be the foundation. Now it has blossomed forth without your even realizing it. It has blossomed because of perseverance, cooperation—because I 'stuck it out.' As far as I could see, however, I was far removed from the poustinia as I thought it should be—as far as the earth from the moon! But lo and behold, *today I discovered that I was always in it.*

"And that is how, in his own good time, the Lord instructed me about my own poustinik vocation. This is what God was preparing in my soul for you. But what has all this to do with you, you the staff workers of Madonna House? You didn't go through a revolution. You didn't seem to be attracted to a life of solitude. You certainly don't seem to be inarticulate or steeped in silence! None of these things were or are yours. Yet, let us look back a little and see what happened to each of you. Yes, let's look back and see what happened to you all.

"First of all, let's take a look at the notion of solitude. Many of you were solitaries in your heart. You yearned for something bigger than yourselves. You did not know that this was solitude. You were sort of different from the people around you, belonging as you did to the Young Christian Workers, CYO, Catholic action of all kinds, or to the new hippies or Jesus people. Even if you didn't belong to any of these groups, there was still some strange kind of solitude in you. You didn't understand it. You didn't know exactly what it was all about, and you were restless. And so, all of you arose, seeking what was not there. Knowing or unknowing, you started on your pilgrimage to the Lord. Yes, that's what you did. You started on the pilgrimage of the Lord.

"So there you were, feeling solitary, going on a pilgrimage of the Lord. But going where? And how? You were walking in silence, a different silence than the one I had. You were in your own land outwardly. You certainly were able to talk to anybody, and you did. Yet, within yourselves there was a strange and awesome silence. You could not communicate too well. For thousands of reasons, you could not communicate too well either with yourselves or with your friends and family. Perhaps this inability to communicate was due to the fact that you hadn't traveled too far yet on your pilgrimage, hadn't accepted completely the silence and the solitude.

"You too were in a strange land, even though you did not know it either. Your pilgrimage led you through this land to Madonna House where I, in turn, was undergoing the same solitude, the same silence, the same feeling of being an alien in a foreign land. You wandered into the strange land of Madonna House, only it wasn't Madonna House. It was the land of Yahweh, of his Son, and of the Holy Spirit. Like Ruth, you began to glean behind the harvesters what was left over. Before long, the Lord himself came and took you by the hand and gave you a scythe and said, 'Go, gather the harvest. The laborers are few and look, the harvest is rich.' And you used the scythe, and you gathered the harvest, and the land ceased to be strange.

"God now extends the same invitation to you as he extended to me. To you also he says, 'I am lonely.' That's what you were, weren't you? Didn't you really start out on your pilgrimage because you were lonely? Now he invites you too to Gethsemane, there to sweat out your struggle with him. He invites you to stand with him before the High Priest, that is to say, before all those who will in some way or other laugh at you, jeer at you, maybe even persecute you.

"When all this has taken place, he will invite you to come with him to Pontius Pilate, into that terrible solitude, into that totally strange land that man must enter before he dies, that predeath land, the last pilgrimage, where strangers will examine you. It may be in Africa, Latin America, some atheistic country. Who knows?

"Finally, he will take you by the hand and lead you to Golgotha to be crucified on the other side of his cross. If you follow him all the way into this poustinia which (I'm almost afraid to say these words) he has brought me to the West to reveal, he will bring you to Golgotha so as to give you the complete, infinite, incredible joy of his resurrection. This joy will be your guide into the new land where there is no solitude, no silence, no strangeness. It will be the final pilgrimage of love toward love, if pilgrimage it can be called. This crucifixion you will undergo with alleluias, because now you will know what it is all about.

"This joy is not only for the hereafter. No. It will be yours now, dearly beloved, this very minute, tomorrow, the day after, as soon as we accept solitude, silence, strange lands, pilgrimages with Christ. When we accept these things we have accepted loneliness, which is none other than the loneliness of Christ. If we can do this, God will give us tools to bring a rich harvest to him and his Church."

15

The Poustinia of the Heart

Well, we have arrived at the end of this book on the poustinia. As for myself, I feel drawn now to a poustinia at Madonna House. I also feel drawn to leave once in a while and go into large cities, to rent a room there in some poor section, and stay there a week or ten days, fasting and praying for that city. Then I shall return to the mountain, only to venture forth again.

This seems to be the last facet of my strange life, of my many vocations in one: single, mother, twice-married, widow, a life of chastity with a husband. I think that the poustinia, as I see it, is the last. The rest I leave to God and to those who will have charge of Madonna House, the house of his Mother which he founded. Amen.

Perhaps it is a little early to say "Amen." For as I sit here and try to rethink and meditate on what I have written about the poustinia—the strange ways of God that brought it to Madonna House—I honestly wonder if I can say "Amen" just yet. My purpose was to explain the poustinia vocation as found in Russia, in my own life, and in the life of Madonna House. I myself have always been attracted to the silence and solitude of God. Even when it became obvious that my vocation was not to be physical silence and solitude, and when I was thrown into the noisiest marketplaces in the world, God showed me how to live out the poustinia ideal. But I have told you all this.

When I spoke the first "Amen" I realized that I hadn't yet given the true picture of the poustinia! I have discussed its Russian origins, I have said a few clumsy words about adapting it to our times, but somehow I haven't yet put my finger on the heart of it. When you come right down to it, the poustinia is not a place at all—and yet it is. It is a state, a vocation, belonging to all Christians by Baptism. *It is the vocation to be a contemplative.*

There will always be "solitaries," or should be. But the essence of the poustinia is that it is a place within oneself, a result of Baptism, where each of us contemplates the Trinity. Within my heart, within me, I am or should be constantly in the presence of God. This is another way of saying that I live in a garden enclosed, where I walk and talk with God (though a Russian would say "where all in me is silent and where I am immersed in the silence of God"). It's as if I were sitting next to God in complete silence, although there are always many other people around. (Like a husband and wife being in a private silence and solitude even though they are at a party and the room is filled with people.) How stumbling words are! How inadequate the similes! Yet the poustinia is something like this to me: a state of contemplating God in silence.

Like the poustinik, I go about God's business all day long. The poustinik enters his poustinia and takes humanity with him. He lifts that humanity before God, with all its pain, sorrows, joys, everything. John Griffin wrote a book called *Black Like Me*. He told how he changed his skin pigmentation into a dark color so that he could really identify with the Black people. A poustinik thus identifies himself with humanity. He *becomes* the Black man, the minority group, the poor, the restless rich—he *is* everyone! By his inner solitude, the poustinik identifies himself with God. Thus identified, he becomes one with the God who became Man.

The poustinia is within, and one is forever immersed in the silence of God, forever listening to the word of God forever repeating it to others in word and deed. Thus, everything that I have said about the physical poustinia, about trying to adapt it to the West, can be said about every Christian everywhere. The poustinia is this inner solitude, this inner immersion in the silence of God. It is through this inner, total identification with humanity and with Christ that every Christian should be living in a state of contemplation. This is the poustinia within oneself.

I don't know if all this makes any sense. It does to me. It is only in identifying with Christ, it is only by plunging into the great silence of God within myself, that I can love and identify with others. It is by listening to the great silence of God, and having this strange, passive dialogue in which I become aware of the silence which is the speech of God— it is only by listening to this that I am able to speak to my brother. It is only by listening to this silence that I can acquire the ingenuity of love, the delicacy of Christ in my human relationships. In this silence I become identified with Christ, I acquire a listening heart.

The poustinia is a state of constantly being in the presence of God because one desires him with a great desire, because in him alone can one rest. The poustinia is walking in this inner solitude, immersed in the silence of God. My life of service and love to my fellowman is simply the echo of this silence and solitude. Inwardly I identify myself with God and with humanity. Jesus Christ himself conducts me into this inner silence, into that solitude which speaks so loudly to the Father under the guidance of the Holy Spirit. Now I am immersed in the Trinity, in the fire of the silence of God (for the silence of God is always fire; his speech is fire). Now I become as one on fire with love of him and of all humanity across the world. Now it is not I who speak. I speak what God tells me to speak. When my immersion into this immense silence has finally caught fire from his words, then I am able to speak. I can speak because his voice is sounding loudly and clearly in my ears, which have been emptied of everything except him. Now only his name is on my heart, constantly; it has become my heartbeat.

This is the poustinia I have been trying to talk about. This is the poustinia I so passionately want to give to everyone. I know that in the poustinia lies the answer that the world is seeking today. The world knows *about* God. Because it only knows *about* him, it can reject him, ignore him, be indifferent to him, recrucify him a thousand times a day in the neighbor. *But if the world knew him through his own revelation of himself to us in the poustinia of our hearts,* then it could not reject him. Once known in this way, he would not be able to be rejected. Then love would enter the world through us. We could speak his word to the world if we lived in the poustinia of our hearts.

For some people, this poustinia of the heart will take on, through the call of God, a definite physical dimension. But it is the poustinia of the heart that I believe is the answer for the modern world. This demands a kenosis. The kenosis begins with the repeating of the Jesus prayer. It begins with a silencing of the noise of my heart. It begins by my folding the wings of the intellect and putting my head into my heart. Only then will the poustinia of the heart become a reality. Then indeed I can go anywhere speak to anybody. make a community of love with my brothers and sisters, meet the stranger (who is simply a friend I haven't met yet). Now, it is not I doing these things, it is Christ within me. My words are not my own. They are the echoes of God's voice that comes to me out of his silence. Now I know how to catch fire from his words and become a fire myself, shedding sparks over the face of the earth. Now I can say that it is not I who live, but Christ lives in me.

I feel that Madonna House will be given an understanding of the poustinia, despite the poor and inadequate way I have told you about it. Perhaps now you will understand why I say that, in order to form a community of love with men, we must make contact with the Trinity, the original community of love. To build such a community we must begin, like the Russian poustinik by emptying ourselves of all our goods and going forth into the solitude and immense silence of God. Material goods, of course, are only the beginning. When you have given up your silver, your gold, your parents, your friends, then you enter into the physical solitude. But you still take with you the "I" that is me, this selfish 'I.' In this inner poustinia you must now empty yourself which is more difficult than giving up everything material. (I think, however, that in the physical poustinia, this "I" dies faster, though it has to die in the inner poustinia of every Christian.

Well, whatever it is, there it is! I don't know what to add. All I know is that I have tried to live the poustinia of the heart in Harlem, in Toronto, wherever I was. I haven't always succeeded. I think that the last phase of my pilgrimage will be the physical solitude and the listening to the silence of God there. Perhaps there God will explain through me, in a manner I am not now aware of, that which I cannot now put into words.

Now, indeed, I must say "Amen." I have nothing more to say. I am empty, spent, yet joyful, for I have tried to explain what to me seems impossible to put into words. I think that many in the future will be able to understand what I have written, and benefit by it. Perhaps there will be some who will arise and go into the real solitude of the mountains of Madonna House in Combermere. There they will listen to God's speech in his wondrous, terrible, gentle, loving, all-embracing silence.

What is Real in Christianity?
DAVID L. EDWARDS

The author strips away the legends from Jesus to show the man who is real, relevant and still fascinating. A clear, confident statement of Christian faith taking account of all criticisms.

The First Christmas
H. J. RICHARDS

Can one really believe in the seventies in such improbable events as the Virgin Birth, the shepherds and the angels, the Magi and the star in the East? Are they just fables? This book suggests that they might be the wrong questions to ask, and may even prevent the reader from arriving at the deeper issues. What these deeper issues are is here explained with clarity, simplicity and honesty.

Wrestling with Christ
LUIGI SANTUCCI

'This is a most unusual book, a prolonged meditation of the life of Christ using many changing literary forms, dialogue, description, addresses to Christ, passages of self-communing. It is written by a Christian passionately concerned that everyone should know Jesus Christ.'   *Catholic Herald*

Journey for a Soul
GEORGE APPLETON

'Wherever you turn in this inexpensive but extraordinarily valuable paperback you will benefit from sharing this man's pilgrimage of the soul.'   *Methodist Recorder*

Also available in Fount Paperbacks

A Historical Introduction to the New Testament
ROBERT GRANT

'This splendid book is a New Testament introduction with a difference . . . All students of the New Testament will welcome this original and courageous study.'

Professor James S. Stewart

The Historical Geography of the Holy Land
G. ADAM SMITH

'A classic which has fascinated and instructed generations of students. This masterpiece among the vast literature on the Bible . . . will continue to delight readers as well as to inform.'

H. H. Rowley

The Dead Sea Scrolls 1947-1969
EDMUND WILSON

'A lucid narrative of the discovery of the scrolls which soon turns into a learned detective story; then an account of the excitement, the consternation and the intrigues.'

V. S. Pritchett, New Statesman

The Gospels and the Jesus of History
XAVIER LEON-DUFOUR

'This book is far more than an introduction to the study of the Gospels. With its detailed study of the Gospels and of the other New Testament books it is an excellent introduction to the Christology of the New Testament.' *William Barclay*

Christology
DIETRICH BONHOEFFER

'The publication of Dietrich Bonhoeffer's *Christology* in English is an exciting event, for here we are given at last not only the basis for his thinking about Christ but the key to his whole theology.'   *T. F. Torrance, Scotsman*

No Rusty Swords
DIETRICH BONHOEFFER

This volume of letters, papers, lecture notes, and pamphlets shows how Bonhoeffer began to fashion new weapons with which to combat the evils of today. A fascinating book.

The Way to Freedom
DIETRICH BONHOEFFER

'Readers of *No Rusty Swords*, the first volume in this trilogy of collected letters, lectures and notes of Dietrich Bonhoeffer, will need no persuasion to follow this inside story of one of the key figures of twentieth-century Christianity.'   *Scotsman*

I Knew Dietrich Bonhoeffer
Ed. RONALD GREGOR SMITH

A rich recollection of reminiscences written by friends, students, colleagues, members of his family, and fellow-conspirators in the plot against Hitler. It shows Bonhoeffer in all aspects of his life, and leaves one with an enduring impression of his charm and integrity.

Also available in Fount Paperbacks

Love and Will
ROLLO MAY

In *Love and Will* the author attacks the prevailing attitude, at the root of permissive society, which flies to the sensation of sex in order to avoid the total commitment of genuine love. He advocates the reintegration of sex with procreative love, true friendship and tenderness.

Power and Innocence
ROLLO MAY

'Encourages one to believe that an intelligent and sophisticated anatomy of our own times is not merely required but actually possible.'   *Guardian*

Relief Without Drugs
AINSLIE MEARES

'Dr Meares describes in detail the simple techniques he advocates to relieve pain and strain, both mental and physical . . . He gives the case histories of patients who have overcome their disabilities and found themselves able to face life with renewed strength and hope.'   *Sunday Times*

Let's Be Human
AINSLIE MEARES

If you wonder about yourself and the way you react – this book explains our reactions on the background of our evolutionary development. The author shows how we must develop 'New Reactions for Old.'

Also available in Fount Paperbacks

Encountering Light
GONVILLE FFRENCH-BEYTAGH

'A book with that extra dimension so easy to recognize and so hard to describe. It is an impressive blend of personal experience and ordered reflection on Christian life in its central aspects.'
The Tablet

Something Beautiful for God
MALCOLM MUGGERIDGE

'An enriching and beautifully produced book. Young and old alike will benefit from reading this book, which is a dedication in itself, while being eminently readable.' *Catholic Truth*

Instrument of Thy Peace
ALAN PATON

'An intensely compelling blend of the mystical and the down-to-earth, this is a personal, devotional anthology.' *The Times*

'Worthy of a permanent place on the short shelf of enduring classics of the life of the Spirit.'
Henry P. Van Dusen, Union Theological Seminary

A Bible Prayer-Book for Today
PETER DE ROSA

A contemporary prayer-book based entirely on the inspired Word of God. There is intense beauty in these prayers but also an exhilarating challenge. This is a book that makes the Bible's message staggeringly relevant to every person's daily life.

THE GOOD NEWS SERIES

Many millions of copies have been sold internationally of *Good News for Modern Man, The New Testament in Today's English Version*. Now for a very large public – including we hope, many who have never read a book about the Bible before – we are proud to publish a brilliant series of introductions, explaining everything that really matters for the modern reader. The contributors are drawn from many traditions in Christianity.

GOOD NEWS IN ACTS introduced by David Edwards

GOOD NEWS IN CORINTHIANS introduced by William Neil

GOOD NEWS IN THE EARLY CHURCH introduced by Martin Marty

GOOD NEWS IN GALATIANS introduced by John Davies

GOOD NEWS IN HEBREWS introduced by Thomas Corbishley

GOOD NEWS IN JOHN introduced by Douglas Webster

GOOD NEWS IN LETTERS OF PAUL introduced by David Read

GOOD NEWS IN LUKE introduced by Wilf Wilkinson

GOOD NEWS IN MARK introduced by Robert Crotty

GOOD NEWS IN MATTHEW introduced by Pierson Parker

GOOD NEWS IN REVELATION introduced by Vernon Sproxton

GOOD NEWS IN ROMANS introduced by Joseph Rhymer

JESUS FOR MODERN MAN by David Edwards